JEWISH CHOICES, JEWISH VOICES

BODY

JEWISH CHOICES, JEWISH VOICES

BODY

EDITED BY
ELLIOT N. DORFF
AND
LOUIS E. NEWMAN

2008 • 5768
Philadelphia

The Jewish Publication Society
2100 Arch Street, 2nd floor
Philadelphia, PA 19103
www.jewishpub.org

Design and Composition by Progressive Information Technologies
Manufactured in the United States of America

08 09 10 11 12   10 9 8 7 6 5 4 3 2 1
ISBN: 978-0-8276-0860-3

Library of Congress Cataloging-in-Publication Data
Jewish choices, Jewish voices / edited by Elliot N. Dorff, Louis E. Newman. — 1st ed.
     v. cm.
   Includes bibliographical references and index.
   Contents: v. 1. The body
   ISBN 978-0-8276-0860-3 (alk. paper)
   1. Jewish ethics.   2. Jews—Identity.   3. Body, Human—Religious aspects—
Judaism.   I. Dorff, Elliot N.   II. Newman, Louis E.

   BJ1285.2.J49 2008
   296.3'6—dc22   2007037402

JPS books are available at discounts for bulk purchases for reading groups, special sales and fundraising purchases. Custom editions, including personalized covers, can be created in larger quantities for special needs. For more information, please contact us at marketing@jewishpub.org or at this address: 2100 Arch Street, Philadelphia, PA 19103.

CONTENTS

Acknowledgments

No series of books such as this comes about without the creative energy and support of many individuals. We wish to thank, first and foremost, Ellen Frankel, editor-in-chief of The Jewish Publication Society, for her vision in first conceiving of this series, and her willingness to entrust it to our editorship. Her wise and patient guidance throughout the process of creating these volumes has been invaluable. The JPS National Council played a critical role early on as the scope and format of the series was in the development stage. Jane Shapiro's expertise as a Jewish educator was instrumental in helping us to formulate the key issues around which to build each volume. Aaron Alexander and Steven Edelman-Blank, both rabbinical students at the University of Judaism (now the American Jewish University), collected, respectively, the traditional and the contemporary Jewish sources for this volume. We are indebted to them for their fine work in locating these materials. The staff of The Jewish Publication Society has been a pleasure to work with at every stage of the production process. We wish to thank especially Carol Hupping, Janet Liss, and Michael Pomante for their professionalism, their responsiveness to all our requests, their patience with all our delays, and their persistent good counsel. Finally, we wish to acknowledge Peter Wieben, a student at Carleton College, for all his work in assembling these volumes and preparing them for publication. His diligence and attention to detail are evident on every page of these books.

Description of the *Jewish Choices, Jewish Voices* Series

This series is intended to provide a forum for discussion of some of the most critical moral issues of our time. Because the Jewish tradition is rich in moral experience and insights, each volume includes Jewish materials from ancient, medieval, and modern sources. And because the Jewish tradition, from its very beginnings, is multivocal, the sources presented deliberately include diverse Jewish perspectives from the past. The process of Jewish wrestling with moral subjects, however, continues in our own day, not only theoretically but concretely and practically. And so each volume presents cases that raise difficult, modern moral issues, together with questions for reflection. We hope that these cases and questions will stimulate you to delve more deeply into the moral issues presented here.

We have also invited a number of modern Jews, representing a variety of backgrounds and Jewish perspectives, either to comment specifically on these cases or to reflect more generally on these moral problems as they come up in their own lives. These modern comments, a symposium of contemporary views and voices, bring new insights to the meaning and relevancy of the sources and take the conversation into new areas worth exploring.

In sum, then, the structure of each book is as follows:

Introduction: The topic of the book, the range of moral issues that it raises, and its import for modern life and for Judaism

I. **Cases and Jewish Sources:** Several cases illustrating some of the specific moral issues involved in this topic, including questions that highlight those issues, followed by ancient Jewish sources and an array of more modern writings relevant to those issues

II. **Symposium:** Contemporary perspectives by Jews on the cases or on the book's topic as they encounter it in their own lives

III. **Conclusion:** A summary of the underlying issues raised in the volume, together with some reflection on other related issues that may arise in the future

Seeing moral issues through a Jewish lens, even one that produces multiple refractions of the Jewish tradition and of Jewish modernity, will, we hope, enable modern Jews to grapple with those issues more intelligently and more sensitively. It is our deepest conviction that these voices from the Jewish tradition and today's Jewish community will invite you to consider your moral choices in a different light. At the very least, they give us all new questions and perspectives to ponder and, more often than not, moral wisdom and guidance.

Elliot N. Dorff
Louis E. Newman
July 2007

Introduction: Body

American and Classical Jewish
Perceptions of the Body

THE TOPIC of this volume, the body, might seem as objective as any topic can be. After all, biologists can describe the features of the human species and the ways they distinguish humans from nonhumans quite precisely. Moreover, researchers can describe typical patterns of development from birth to death. There is a range of what are considered to be "normal" human traits. For instance, there are average weight and height ranges for men and for women, and people falling outside either of those ranges are considered to be atypical. Furthermore, there are always cases that test the borders of what we generally consider normal. Although most humans, for example, are either male or female, some have characteristics of both. Most humans have two legs, but some are born with only one or lose one or both of their legs during life. Most human beings are born with their own internal organs, but some share one or more organs with a conjoined twin. Still, even with all these variations, we might claim that the human body is as concrete as tables or chairs.

But the human body is not nearly as matter-of-fact as that. Different cultures train us how to perceive our bodies as well as how to reach moral judgments about the way we treat them. To illustrate this, let's compare prevailing American perspectives on the body with a classical Jewish view. Without delving into the complexities of either point of view, according to American thought and law, I own my body. I may not use it to harm someone else; and so, for example, if I have an infectious disease, the government may put me under quarantine and insist that I stay in my house for a period of time. As long as I do not harm anyone else, however, I may be as scrupulous or as careless in the care of my body as I choose. In fact, as the *Nancy Cruzan* decision of the U.S. Supreme Court held, any adult may refuse all medical treatment. Government or medical authorities may try to stop me from committing suicide; and, as a pair of U.S. Supreme Court decisions held, I do not have the constitutional right to procure aid in committing suicide or to help someone else do so. Short of that, however, I have complete authority to determine how much I eat, exercise, wash, and sleep.

In American thought, the purpose of my body is the pragmatic one of supporting the various activities of my life. As a result, I have a duty to engage in proper diet, exercise, hygiene, and sleep for pragmatic purposes—so that I will feel good, look good, and avoid health problems; cost my employer, health insurer, or family less in health care; participate with friends in sports and other physical fitness activities; and enhance my ability to get jobs.

The broad outlines of Judaism's view of the body are substantially different. Along with my parents, God is a co-creator of my body. In the Rabbis' understanding of the process, however, my parents contributed only the physical materials out of which I came to be; it was God who breathed life into that matter. So God is the creator of my life and, as its creator, God owns my body throughout my life and even in death. If this connection between creation and ownership may not seem obvious to moderns, it is partially because of the Industrial Revolution, which divided the tasks of creation of most things in our lives among many different people. Consider, however, those areas of our lives where only one individual or a small group of people create something for illustrations of how creation confers ownership—for example, the painter of a painting, the composer of a piece of music, or the author of a book.

As owner of my body, God can and does make demands as to how I use it. I may not, for example, commit suicide because that would be destroying that which does not belong to me, as well as diminishing the image of God in the world, for each of us is created in the image of God. I may take reasonable risks in living my life, but not extraordinary risks, for "endangering [oneself] is prohibited more stringently than violating the [other] prohibitions [of the Torah]" (Babylonian Talmud, Hullin 10a). Exactly where that line is drawn admits some variation, for some people are more able to handle some risks (e.g., in skiing) than others, and some rabbis interpreting Jewish law demand more caution than others (e.g., in responding to the question of whether a Jew may smoke). In the end, though, I have a fiduciary relationship with God with respect to my body—that is, God entrusts it to me for the duration of my life on the condition that I take care of it. So, for example, I may not eat a half gallon of ice cream every night of the week even if I want to do so and do not care about the pragmatic results—that I will gain 100 pounds in no time and thereby endanger my health and cease to look good or feel good. Conversely, I have a positive duty to God to practice habits of proper diet, exercise, hygiene, and sleep, whether or not I want to do so. Along these lines, Jewish law prescribes that I must live in a town where there is a physician, for otherwise I could not obtain the expert help I need to avoid and overcome illness. Furthermore, I must do what the doctor orders to maintain my health. I may choose among several viable medical alternatives; and in the last stages of life that may include withholding or withdrawing machines, medications, and—according to some—artificial nutrition and hydration. But I must have regular checkups, consult a doctor if I get sick, and do what is medically advisable. The goal of taking care of my body in Judaism is, as Maimonides (an important twelfth-century rabbi, doctor, and philosopher) put it, so that I can be in a position to fulfill the Torah's commandments. Bad health habits and illness impede my ability to do that. Because the goal of my life is to live in covenant with God and thus to fix the world, I must take care of my body in order to enable myself to accomplish those tasks. Because that is the goal, age and experience are prized.

Even this brief overview of how American and Jewish traditions regard the body illustrates how different they are and how important it is to consider ultimate viewpoints and values when thinking about how we use our bodies. This lesson is embedded in the very word "religion." *Lig* comes from the Latin word for "connection," suggesting that religions—and many secular philosophies as well—are designed to link us to our family, our community, the broader human community, the environment, and to what transcends human experience, imaged in the Western religions as God and in the Eastern religions in other ways. The prefix *re* suggests that religion "binds (us) again" to all the people and communities in our life, presumably after moments of disconnection. Such moments are especially common in young adults, who often leave behind their family's religious moorings, only to reconnect later, once they have achieved a greater sense of identity and independence.

Every religion provides a broad perspective, a "Grand Canyon view," as it were, about who we are and who we ought to be. Although most religions or secular philosophies overlap to some extent, they exhibit a remarkable range of values. Even regarding something as basic as rules about homicide, views range from complete pacifism on one end of the spectrum, to idealizing military exploits on the other.

So cultural perspectives, even about things as concrete and factual as the body, greatly influence how we feel about and act toward our body.

Furthermore, the fact that American and classical Jewish views of the body differ as much as they do means that American Jews may need to choose between the teachings of these two traditions with which they identify when the views conflict. For many, that will not mean always preferring one over the other. Rather, it will mean assessing each tradition's approach to a given issue in order to decide which to choose, or sometimes, balancing one against the other in order to adopt a position that respects both or lands somewhere in between. The value of such comparisons is that they give American Jews an opportunity to learn from both these inherited traditions so that they can harvest from them as they form their own, mature moral thinking about significant issues in their lives.

Male and Female Bodies

Human bodies, of course, are gendered. This fact immediately raises a whole set of issues regarding sexual activities, but this volume will not deal with sex; that will be the topic of a separate volume in this series.

The gendered quality of human bodies raises a number of issues concerning the similar and different ways in which men and women perceive their bodies. Both men and women these days worry about obesity; but for reasons not well understood, it is primarily women who suffer from anorexia and bulimia. Both men and women want to be fit, but it is primarily men who care more about bulging arm and leg muscles. Both men and women, especially in their twenties and thirties, want to look sexy; but because biology distinguishes the sexual anatomy of men and women, this translates into very different concerns for men and women.

From the time of the very earliest written sources, the factor of human gender has also produced literature and law about how each gender understands and interacts with the other. The very first chapter of the Torah says, literally, "And God created man in His image, in the image of God He created him; male and female He created them." (Genesis 1:27). Although that could be read to mean that God created humankind to be both male and female from the beginning, the Rabbis, reading the number and gender of the nouns and pronouns literally, suggest that God first created one person who was androgynous. The second chapter of Genesis, however, asserts that God first created a male human being from the dust, and then created a female from the man's side in order to be his helpmate. This second account, and the Garden of Eden story that follows in chapter three, assert that man is first in the order of Creation and is designed/meant to reign over woman. So even the opening chapters of Genesis give us conflicting understandings of human gender and of their proper relationship.

How men and women should relate to each other is a very old theme, and it is an ongoing and pervasive one. Indeed, male–female relationships affect a multitude of areas in life, including, among others, how men and women think about members of their own gender in contrast to those of the opposite gender, how they speak to each other (can you tell dirty jokes or use swear words with equal abandon when members of the opposite sex are present?) and treat each other (is chivalry really dead?), what they look for in a mate or in a partner at work, how they date, and the expectations that men and women have of each other in marriage and in child rearing.

Until very recently in both American and Jewish law, and still today in some quarters, these presumptions about each gender had direct ramifications for both American and Jewish law. The presumptions about males and females affect public policies, like eligibility for jobs and leadership positions, and people's private lives, like legal and ritual forms of marriage and divorce and rules for deciding child custody disputes.

Although society has always made distinctions between men and women, since the twentieth century—especially since Betty Friedan's *The Feminine Mystique* (1963)—such gender distinctions have come under intense scrutiny as feminism has challenged the legitimacy of making distinctions on the basis of gender alone in shaping employment, law, or public policy. Even restricting marriage to a man and a woman is being increasingly challenged in both American and Jewish circles.

New attitudes toward gender roles are immensely liberating for both men and women, for now each person is "free to be you and me," as the popular song from the 1970s put it—that is, free to aspire to any position, free to redefine the duties of marriage in partnership with one's spouse, and so on. But discarding traditional definitions of what it means to be a man or a woman can raise challenging questions for both men and women about their own gender identity. Their answers also affect how they raise their sons and daughters.

As gendered beings, we are deeply affected by all of these old and new male–female issues. It therefore should be no surprise that even when the issue at hand is not directly about how men and women interact with members of the opposite sex, it often has a gendered component, one that we must be aware of if we are going to treat the particular moral issue we are discussing adequately.

Although it is important to recognize the role of gender in one's moral calculus, it is also important not to exaggerate it. Gender is not always pertinent. To pretend that issues of gender underlie absolutely every moral problem distorts matters just as much as claiming that gender plays no role in such problems. The trick is to remember that we are both human and gendered. Sometimes the focus is on our common humanity; other times, we are separated by our genders.

Multiple Classical and Modern Jewish Perspectives

Finally, in addressing the moral matters in this book and the others in this series, it is important to remember that contemporary American Jews balance not only their Jewish and American identities but also the classical Jewish tradition and multiple, modern expressions of it. To say honestly and accurately that "Judaism says . . ." is hard enough when both speaker and listener (or writer and reader) agree that there is only a single version of classical Judaism. But this claim to a monolithic Judaism is disingenuous: Both the Bible and the Talmud resonate with many, many voices articulating often diverse points of view. The very feistiness of the tradition, its argumentativeness and respect for differences of opinion is, in our view, one of its chief attractions and an important source of its wisdom.

If one is trying to articulate the assertions of modern Judaism, then one has to be especially careful. It is not just by accident that there are four separate movements within North American Judaism—alphabetically: Conservative, Orthodox, Reconstructionist, and Reform (with Renewal Judaism in the process of emerging as yet another approach). We cannot legitimately speak about "Jewish bioethics," "Jewish sexual ethics," or "Jewish business ethics" as if there were a single, unambiguous perspective on these subjects. We must instead talk more humbly about "*a* Jewish approach" rather than "*the* Jewish approach," and then demonstrate that the position we are taking is rooted in Jewish sources, concepts, and values, making legitimate our claim that our position is indeed a Jewish approach. Recognizing this reality has led us in this and every other volume to include a variety of authors with many different Jewish beliefs and approaches to comment on the issues we have raised.

This is not to say that either classical or modern Judaism is incoherent, that anything goes. On many issues, in fact, it is fairly easy to describe positions held by most Jewish authorities, past and present. This holds true even for some distinctly modern issues, such as embryonic stem cell research. The official positions of all four modern Jewish movements not only permit this research but actively encourage it. On some other matters, we find only two or three positions that have divided Jews since antiquity. It is only on a small number of issues that Jews differ radically among themselves; no one position can claim to be mainstream. Such wide diversion usually occurs vis-à-vis the cutting-edge moral issues of a given era, like the ones of the last generation that dealt with how to respond to revolutionary medical advances and to changing gender roles, and the ones emerging in this generation, including the status of homosexual relations and issues of privacy and security raised by the Internet and other technological advances.

As we now explore some important issues raised by our relationship to our own physicality, we turn to ancient, medieval, and modern Jewish perspectives to guide us in making our decisions. One of the great strengths of the Jewish tradition is that it encourages each of us to make this tradition our own. Toward that end, the tradition has preserved multiple positions on any given issue. Even when rabbinic authority prefers one to all others, it nevertheless presumes that Jews will continue to argue about whether and why this should be the official stance. Just as Abraham, Moses, Jeremiah, and Job all argued with God, Jews continue that noble tradition—and argue with each other as well.

PART I

⤸

CASE STUDIES AND JEWISH SOURCES

First Case Study: Body Weight and Diet Choices

A BIGAIL, WHO is 30 years old, is employed as a sales representative for a pharmaceutical company, and her skills make her a likely candidate for a senior sales position, giving her larger accounts. She is, however, 50 pounds over her ideal weight. She has tried to lose weight a number of times, but has proven unable to do so. Her superiors tell her that they can never promote her to that position at her present weight because, frankly, it will turn off potential clients. Moreover, they do not want to invest more money in training her, given that her unhealthy behavior lowers her life expectancy, leads to many sick days, and adds to their health-care costs. Abigail is married to Barry, who has no problems with Abigail's weight; in fact, Abigail was more or less the same size when they first met. Abigail is quite energetic and very well organized, and so she manages to share household duties and child-raising tasks with Barry with little difficulty and with great skill. At the insistence of her employer, she sees a doctor, who discovers that Abigail has high blood pressure and diabetes, which are often signs of worse things to come. Learning of these diagnoses, her employer tells her that, as a condition of her eligibility for promotion, Abigail must do something to lose weight. Her boss even offers to share the cost of Abigail's enrolling in whatever programs she thinks will help her accomplish this goal.

Questions

1. Does Abigail have a duty to care for her body? If so, to whom? To herself? Her family? Her employer? Her clients? The insurance company? God?

2. To what extent does her employer's demand to lose weight violate her individual rights to live her life as she wants, especially because she knows fully about the risks that she is assuming?

3. If there were no employment issue and she did not have children, would she still have a duty to choose a healthy lifestyle? If so, what are the grounds of this duty and to whom does it apply?

4. Is Abigail entitled to do whatever she wants in order to improve her appearance—for example, undergo cosmetic surgery or liposuction?

Traditional Jewish Sources Relevant to All Cases

The Duty to Care for One's Own Body

1. Deuteronomy 10:14

Mark, the heavens to their uttermost reaches belong to the Lord your God, the earth and all that is on it!

2. Deuteronomy 4:9

But take utmost care and watch yourselves scrupulously, so that you do not forget the things that you saw with your own eyes and so that they do not fade from your mind as long as you live. And make them known to your children and to your children's children.

3. Shulchan Arukh, Hoshen Mishpat 427:8

It is a positive commandment to be very careful and guard oneself from any life-threatening obstacle as it is said, " . . . take utmost care and watch yourselves scrupulously" (Deut. 4:9).

4. Midrash Leviticus Rabbah 34:3

When he [Hillel] finished the lesson with his students, he accompanied them part of the way. They said to him, "Master, where are you going?" "To perform a religious duty [i.e., to take a bath]." "Which religious duty?" He answered them, "If somebody appointed to scrape and clean the statues of kings in the theatres and circuses is paid to do the work and furthermore is considered noble for doing so, how much more so should I, created in the divine image and likeness, take care of my body!"

5. Maimonides, *Mishneh Torah,* Laws of Ethics (De'ot) 3:3

He who regulates his life in accordance with the laws of medicine with the sole motive of maintaining a sound and vigorous physique and begetting children to do his work and labor for his benefit is not following the right path. A man should aim to maintain physical health and vigor in order that his soul may be upright, in a condition to know God. . . .

Whoever throughout his life follows this course will be continually serving God, even while engaged in business and even during sexual relations, because his purpose in all that he does will be to satisfy his needs so as to have a sound body with which to serve God. Even when he sleeps and seeks repose to calm his mind and rest his body so as not to fall sick and be incapacitated from serving God, his sleep is his service to the Almighty.

6. Babylonian Talmud Yoma 85b

Rabbi Eliezer said, "If circumcision, which pertains to only one of the two-hundred-and-forty-eight limbs of the body, takes precedence over the prohibitions of Shabbat, all the more so the saving of the *entire* body should take precedence over the prohibitions of Shabbat."(After the Talmud offers a number of proofs for this, this statement is offered:)

Said Rabbi Yehudah in the name of Rabbi Shmuel, "If I had been there, I would have offered an even finer proof text, specifically, "He shall live by them" (Leviticus 18:5) [that is to say, one should live by the commandments] and not die by them.

The Duty to Avoid Danger to Oneself and Others

7. Babylonian Talmud Hullin 10a

Regulations concerning danger to life are more imperative than ritual prohibitions.

8. Mishnah Bava Kamma 8:6 (90b)

Rabbi Akiba said: "A person is not permitted to harm himself."

9. Shulchan Arukh, Yoreh De'ah 116:5 (Rama)

One should distance oneself from things that may lead to danger, for a danger to life is more serious than a [religious] prohibition—and one should be more worried about a possible danger to life than a possible [transgression] of a prohibition. Therefore, the Sages prohibited one to walk in a place of danger, such as close to a leaning/shaky wall or alone at night. They also prohibited drinking water from streams at night or placing one's mouth on a flowing pipe of water to drink, for these things may lead to danger . . . All of these things are intended to avoid danger, and one who is concerned with his health will avoid them. And it is prohibited to rely on a saving miracle, or to endanger oneself in a like way.

10. Babylonian Talmud Berachot 32b–33a

We have learned in an early rabbinic statement:

A pious man was once saying the Silent Prayer [Amidah] while traveling. An officer approached him and offered him a greeting, but [the pious man] did not greet him in return. [The officer] waited for the pious man to finish his Prayer. After he finished his Prayer, the officer said to him, "Fool! Does your Torah not state, 'But take utmost care and watch yourselves scrupulously' (Deut. 4:9), and it also states, 'For your own sake, therefore, be most careful' (Deut 4:15). [That is, the Torah demands that you protect your life.] When I offered you a greeting, why did you not greet me back? If I had to cut your head off with a sword, who would have demanded restitution for your blood?"

[The pious man] replied, "Hold on, as I will appease you with an argument. If you were standing before a human king, and a friend came to greet you—would you have greeted him back?

[The officer] replied, "No!"

[The pious man continued] "And if you indeed would have returned the greeting to him, what would they have done to you?"

[The officer] said to him, "They would have cut off my head with a sword!"

[The pious man] replied, "Is this not an *a fortiori* argument? Just as you were standing before a human king, who is alive one day and dead the next [and did not return a greeting], so too, I, who stood before the King of Kings, the Holy One, blessed be He, who lives eternally— all the more so [that I should not stop my Prayer, even if a dangerous situation presents itself]."

The officer was immediately appeased, and the pious man went home in peace.

11. Shulchan Arukh, Hoshen Mishpat 427:10

Anyone who transgresses these matters [health concerns], saying: "I will endanger myself, what business is that of anyone else?" or "I'm not concerned with such things," prepare for him lashes. Anyone who *is* careful about such matters [health concerns], a blessing shall come to him.

12. Midrash Leviticus Rabbah 4:6

Rabbi Shimon bar Yohai taught, "This is like some people who were sitting in a boat. One of them picked up a drill and started to drill a hole beneath himself. The other said to him, 'What are you doing?' He responded, 'What do you care? Am I not drilling under my own place?'

13. Deuteronomy 22:8

When you build a new house, you shall make a parapet for your roof, so that you do not bring bloodguilt on your house if anyone should fall from it.

14. Babylonian Talmud Bava Batra 18b

The Rabbis are of the opinion that it is the responsibility of the owner of a hazard to remove it.

15. Babylonian Talmud Bava Kamma 15b

Rabbi Nathan said: How do we know that a person should not keep a vicious dog in his home, or keep an insecure ladder in his home? Because the Torah says, "You should not bring bloodguilt on your house" (Deuteronomy 22:8).

16. Babylonian Talmud Ta'anit 11a

A person should always measure his actions as if the Holy One resides within him.

17. Babylonian Talmud Avodah Zarah 30b

R. Eliezer said: One may eat grapes and figs at night without being concerned [about the danger inherent in it], because [Scripture] says: *God protects the simple* (Psalms 116:6).

18. Babylonian Talmud Shabbat 129b

Why is blood-letting permitted on Fridays, if on Fridays the planet Mars predominates at even daytime hours [hence rendering these hours unusually dangerous]? Because the multitude are accustomed to doing this at that time, it may be considered permissible because "the Lord protects the simple" (Psalms 116:6).

The Duty to Rescue Others

19. Leviticus 19:16

Do not stand idly by the blood of your neighbor.

20. Rashi to Leviticus 19:16

To watch his death when you could have saved him. For instance, if one is drowning in a river or if a wild beast or armed bandit is attacking him, [this verse requires you to come to his rescue].

21. Mishnah Sanhedrin 4:5

For this reason Adam was created alone: to teach you that destroying a single life is to destroy a whole world, even as to save a life is to save a whole world. And for the sake of the peace of creation, that no one should say to another, "My ancestor was greater than yours." And so that heretics cannot say, "There are many powers in heaven." And to proclaim the greatness of the Blessed Holy One, for when a person makes many coins with one die, they all look alike, but the Blessed Holy One stamps every human being with the die of the first Adam, and none resembles the other. For this reason, each and every person must declare, "For my sake the world was created."

22. Babylonian Talmud Yoma 85a

If a building fell upon a person [on the Sabbath] and it is unknown as to whether he is there or not, whether he is alive or dead, or whether he is a Jew or a gentile—they clear away the debris that is on him [to save his life despite the ban on destroying a building on the Sabbath]. . . . If they found him alive, they remove the remaining debris that is on him.

If they found him alive they remove the remaining debris that is on him:

Is that not obvious!? Actually, this statement comes to teach us an additional point, namely, that even if he has only a short time to live, they remove the remaining debris.

God and Physicians as Agents of Healing

22. Exodus 15:26

He said, "If you will heed the Lord your God diligently, doing what is upright in His sight, giving ear to His commandments and keeping all His laws, then I will not bring upon you any of the diseases that I brought upon the Egyptians, for I, the LORD, am your healer."

23. Rabbeinu Nissim to Sanhedrin 84b

All types of healing are dangerous for the patient because it is possible the doctor will make a mistake concerning a specific drug/procedure and kill the patient.

24. Rabbi Abraham Ibn Ezra, Commentary to Exodus 21:19

He must pay for his idleness and his cure [when he strikes another and the victim does not die—Exodus 21:19]: This only gives permission to doctors to heal outer wounds and blemishes, but internal injuries are left for God to heal.

Traditional Sources

1. Proverbs 31:30–31

30. Grace is deceptive,
Beauty is illusory;
It is for her fear of the Lord
31. That a woman is to be praised.
Extol her for the fruit of her hand,
And let her works praise her in the gates.

2. Babylonian Talmud Berachot 58b

At the sight of beautiful creatures and beautiful trees, one should say, "Blessed be He who has such in His world."

3. Babylonian Talmud Shabbat 50b

A man may scrape off pieces of feces and scabs on his flesh [on the Sabbath] because of his pain [that they cause]. However, if [one of these things is done] for beautification [on the Sabbath], it is prohibited [due to the prohibition for a man to groom himself as a woman grooms herself].

4. Tosafot to Shabbat 50b, s.v. *because of his pain*

And if there is no physical pain, but the person is embarrassed to be among other people, it is permitted—because there is no greater pain than this [embarrassment].

5. Babylonian Talmud Bava Batra 18b

The Rabbis maintain that it is the responsibility of the owner of a hazard to remove it.

6. Babylonian Talmud Sanhedrin 20a

'Beauty is deceitful . . . It is the fear of the Lord whereby one is adorned' (Proverbs 31:30). The verse applies to the generation of R. Judah son of R. Ilai, of which is it said: [Though their poverty was so great that] six of R. Judah's disciples had to make do with one cloak for all of them, yet they occupied themselves with Torah.

7. Babylonian Talmud Avodah Zarah 12a

In every place the Sages prohibited [an act] due to appearance, they prohibited [that act] even in one's innermost rooms [in private].

8. Maimonides, *Mishneh Torah,* Laws of Ethics (De'ot) 3:2

Similarly, when one eats, drinks, and has sexual relations—it should not be done simply for the pleasure alone, for then [one might come to] eat and drink only sweet foods and have sexual relations only for pleasure. Rather, pay attention to eat and drink in order to keep the entire body healthy. Therefore, one should not eat anything the palate desires, like a dog or a donkey; rather, eat [also] things that are good for the body—whether they are sweet or bitter. Also, one should not eat things that are bad for the body, even if they are sweet to the palate. . . .

9. Maimonides, *Mishneh Torah,* Laws of Ethics (De'ot) 4:15

Overeating is considered like poison to one's body—this is the essence of sickness. The majority of sicknesses that befall a person are from eating harmful foods, filling one's belly and overeating—even healthy foods.

Contemporary Sources

Source 1

Since men have used women's "beauty" as a form of currency in circulation among men, ideas about "beauty" have evolved since the Industrial Revolution side by side with ideas about money, so that the two are virtual parallels in our consumer economy. A woman looks like a million dollars, she's a first-class beauty, her face is her fortune. In the bourgeois marriage markets of the last century, women learned to understand their own beauty as part of this economy.

By the time the women's movement had made inroads into the labor market, both women and men were accustomed to having beauty evaluated as wealth. Both were unprepared for the striking development that followed: As women demanded access to power,

10

the power structure used the beauty myth materially to undermine women's advancement.

—Naomi Wolf, *The Beauty Myth: How Images of Beauty Are Used against Women* (New York: Anchor Books, 1992), 20.

Source 2

It is a truism, for instance, that a few clothes are more shocking than none. But for women especially, bras, panties, bathing suits, and other stereotypical gear are visual reminders of a commercial, idealized feminine image that our real and diverse female bodies can't possibly fit. Without those visual references, each individual woman's body demands to be accepted on its own terms. We stop being comparatives. We begin to be unique.

—Gloria Steinem, "In Praise of Women's Bodies," *Ms. Magazine* (April 1981) reprinted in *Outrageous Acts and Everyday Rebellions* (New York: Signet, 1986), 183.

Source 3

For Judaism, God owns everything, including our bodies. God lends our bodies to us for the duration of our lives, and we return them to God when we die. Consequently, neither men nor women have the right to govern their bodies as they will; since God created our bodies and owns them, God can and does restrict how we use our bodies according to the rules articulated in Jewish law.

One set of rules requires us to take responsible care of our bodies. Just as we would be obliged to take reasonable care of an apartment on loan to us, so too we have the duty to take care of our own bodies. Rules of good hygiene, sleep, exercise, and diet are not just words to the wise designed for our comfort and longevity but rather commanded acts that we owe God. So, for example, Hillel regards bathing as a commandment (*mitzvah*), and Maimonides includes directives for good health in his code of law, considering them just as obligatory as other positive duties like caring for the poor.

—Elliot N. Dorff, *Matters of Life and Death: A Jewish Approach to Modern Medical Ethics* (Philadelphia: The Jewish Publication Society, 1998), 15.

Source 4

In separate empirical analyses using three sets of household data, we find some evidence of a positive impact of workers' looks on their earnings. The evidence in each sample alone is suggestive but not very strong. When the three samples are combined, however, sample sizes become sufficient to make some fairly clear inferences about the role of beauty in the labor market. Other things equal, wages of people with below-average looks are lower than those of average-looking workers; and there is a premium in wages for good-looking people that is slightly smaller than this penalty. The penalty and premium may be higher for men, but these gender differences are not large. There is also some evidence that the labor market sorts the best looking people into occupations where their looks are productive.

—Daniel S. Hamermesh and Jeff E. Biddle, "Beauty and the Labor Market," *The American Economic Review* 84, no. 5 (December 1994), 1192.

Source 5

Keeping healthy can also become a moral issue. Individuals are made to feel guilty for getting sick. People shake their heads disapprovingly over those who "don't take care of themselves." In many cases, this amounts to blaming the victim; it shows a failure to recognize both the social and the economic influences on health habits and the complexity of illness. With personal habits, too, a certain tendency to judge creeps in: "She *should* get more exercise, stop eating so much sugar." Even when these are matters of personal choice, a moralistic healthism is inappropriate. And it doesn't help people change, even when they may want to.

—Wendy Sanford, Nancy Miriam Hawley, and Jane Pincus, "Introduction to Part One: Taking Care of Ourselves," revised by Jennifer Yanco and Judy Norsigian in *Our Bodies, Ourselves for the New Century: A Book by and for Women* (New York: Touchstone, 1998), 30.

Source 6

Jewish law prohibits us from causing physical injury (*chabalah*) to ourselves without sufficient justification. The debate over cosmetic surgery within the tradition accordingly centers upon the precise definitions we give to this prohibition. Some assert that, so long as a particular cosmetic surgery is not unusually risky and is being contemplated for honorable reasons, the surgery does not violate the guidelines set forth by our sources and sages. Others, however, argue that cosmetic surgery, like all other medical treatment, is permitted only for *refu'ah,* for healing, for legitimate *medical* purposes. The desire to improve one's physical appearance is, in and of itself, not such a "legitimate medical purpose." Indeed, it may be viewed as an act of arrogance, a desecration of the human form, and an example of misplaced values: with all the important work that we need to do in the field of medicine and healing, is the enhancement of physical beauty truly a proper end to which we ought to apply our knowledge and resources?

Reform [Judaism's] responsa view the latter position as the better interpretation of Jewish teaching. Our reverence for the sanctity of the human body prevents us from the capricious manipulation of its form, and surgery merely to improve one's physical appearance should be discouraged. There are, or course, exceptions to this general rule. We believe that reconstructive surgery, the restoration of one's appearance to an approximation of its former state, is a proper medical objective and not merely cosmetic. Surgery to correct what are generally regarded as physical deformities is also permissible. Moreover, for some persons "mere" cosmetic surgery may serve as a useful medical purpose in enhancing a sense of psychological and emotional well-being. This is a determination which must be made in each individual case, although we think the argument is too frequently raised and too easily exaggerated. As we understand it, Judaism admonishes us to place less emphasis than we are prone to do on material values and to concentrate upon the development of deeper and more lasting measurements of self-worth and satisfaction. We ought to resist undertaking surgery intended solely for the improvement of physical appearance.

—Mark Washofsky, *Jewish Living: A Guide to Contemporary Reform Practice* (New York: UAHC Press, 2001), 259.

Second Case Study: Tattoos

Chuck is 24 years old, out of college, single, and employed as a paralegal in a law firm. He began tattooing parts of his body as a teenager and has continued to add tattoos from time to time in the years since. At his parents' insistence, however, he has had tattoos applied only by a professional tattoo artist, who takes ample precautions to avoid infections and other medical complications. He now wants to become more observant and to live a more traditional Jewish life. He has discovered, however, that the Torah prohibits tattooing (Leviticus 19:28, 21:5; Deuteronomy 14:1), although it seems to be based on a biblical ban on ancient Canaanite cultic practices related to warding off death or mourning the dead. Chuck's choices to tattoo himself were based solely on the belief that tattoos make his body more attractive.

Questions

1. Is there any compelling reason for Chuck to give up his long-standing practice of tattooing himself?

2. Does it change the situation if Chuck is in a serious relationship with a woman who (a) likes his tattoos or (b) very much dislikes them?

3. What duties does Chuck have to respect his own body and care for it? Assuming that tattooing his body does not harm either himself or others, should this behavior be construed as a form of respecting his body, disrespecting it, or simply a matter of personal discretion?

Traditional Sources

[Note to readers: Refer also to "Traditional Jewish Sources Relevant to All Cases Studies," on page 3.]

1. Exodus 19:5

Now then, if you will obey Me faithfully and keep my covenant, you shall be my treasured people among all the peoples. Indeed, all the earth is mine.

2. Leviticus 19:28

You shall not make gashes in your flesh for the dead, or incise any marks on yourselves: I am the LORD.

3. Rashi to Leviticus 19:28

[This prohibits] an inscription etched and sunken that cannot ever be erased, for one etched it with a needle and it remains permanently black.

4. Mishnah Makkot 3:6

With regard to one who tattoos his skin, [if] he made a mark [an incision in his skin] but did not tattoo it in [that is, did not fill it in with ink, or] tattooed it in [that is, made ink marks on the surface of his skin]

14

but did not make a mark [so that the process of tattooing was not completed] —he is not liable. He is liable [only] when he marks *and* tattoos with ink or eye paint or anything that leaves a [permanent] mark. Rabbi Simon ben Judah says in the name of Rabbi Simon, "He is liable only when he writes the name of God, as it is written, "nor incise any marks on yourselves: I am the LORD (Leviticus 19:28)."

5. Babylonian Talmud Makkot 21a

Rabbi Aha ben Rava said to Rabbi Ashi: Does that [the remark of R. Simon ben Judah in Source 4 above] mean [he is liable for flogging] if he will actually write, "I am the LORD?" He answered [R. Ashi to R. Aha], "No—it is as Bar Kappara taught in an early rabbinic statement [*baraita*]: 'He is liable for flogging only if he inscribes the name of another God, as it is written, "nor incise any marks on yourselves: I am the LORD," [i.e., there is no other].

6. Rashi to Makkot 21a

The essence of not writing a name of God is the prohibition of worshipping other gods. However, one should not make any tattoo whatsoever. This is even according to the opinion of Rabbi Simon [in Source 4 above]. According to him, though, [one is] liable for lashes [only] for tattooing the name of a god.

7. Jerusalem Talmud Nedarim 9:1

Do you think that what the Torah prohibits is not sufficient for you, such that you take upon yourself additional prohibitions? [With respect to the discussion in the Mishnah above perhaps, we should not add onto these prohibitions by prohibiting modern tattoos that are not idolatrous.]

8. Babylonian Talmud Nazir 19a

What is the meaning of the verse, "He [the Nazarite—see Numbers 6:11] shall atone for him for having sinned against the soul"? Against which soul did he sin? Rather, because he deprived himself of wine. Now, there is an *a priori* argument: If the one who deprived himself *only* of wine is called "a sinner," then how much the more so someone who deprives himself of all things.

9. Maimonides, *Mishneh Torah,* Laws of Idolatry 12:11

The [prohibition] of tattooing that is biblically derived is making an incision in one's flesh and filling the incision with eye paint, ink, or

15

any dye that leaves an imprint. This was the practice of idolaters who [permanently] marked their bodies for the sake of their idol worship. Basically, [they understood this to be] that they are likened to servants sold to the idol and designated to serve it.

When one makes an imprint with one of the substances [listed above], the punishment of lashes is carried out, whether it was a man or a woman.

If one wrote but did not dye, or dyed but did not write [by incising in the flesh]—this person is not liable, as it is written (Lev. 19:28), "or incise any marks."

To whom does this [prohibition] apply? To the one who is performing the tattooing, but the one who is tattooed by others is not liable unless he helped the tattooer [so that it is] as if he tattooed too. However, if the one being tattooed did not perform the action, [the punishment] of lashes is not applied.

Contemporary Sources

Source 1

In our day, the prohibition against all forms of tattooing, regardless of their intent, should be maintained. In addition to the fact that Judaism has a long history of distaste for tattoos, tattooing becomes even more distasteful when confronted with a contemporary secular society that is constantly challenging the Jewish concept that we are created *b'tzelem elohim,* "in the Image of God," and that our bodies are to be viewed as a precious gift on loan from God, to be entrusted into our care and not our personal property to do with as we choose. Voluntary tattooing, even if not done for idolatrous purposes, expresses a negation of this fundamental Jewish perspective. . . . But, however distasteful we may find the practice, there is no basis for restricting burial to a Jew who violates this prohibition or even limiting their participation in synagogue ritual. The fact that someone may have violated the laws of kashrut at some point in their life or violated the laws of Shabbat would not merit such sanctions; the prohibition against tattooing is certainly no worse. It is only because of the permanent nature of the tattoo that the transgression is still visible.

—Alan B. Lucas, "Tattooing and Body Piercing." www.rabbinicalassembly
.org/teshuvot/docs/19912000/lucas_tattooing.pdf (accessed June 23, 2006).

Source 2

The reasons Jews are getting tattooed are as varied as the designs they proudly—and often defiantly—display.

Riqi Kosovske, 35, a third-year rabbinical student at the Reform movement's Hebrew Union College-Jewish Institute of Religion in Los Angeles, has a hamsa tattooed on her ankle. A Middle Eastern and Jewish good-luck symbol featuring an open hand, the marking epitomizes her conflict between traditional Judaism and creative, expressive spirituality.

It's also a constant reminder of her struggle.

When she got the tattoo, she was leaving freewheeling Berkeley and her life as a Jewish educator for a new beginning in Israel and rabbinical school.

"Something about the hamsa feels very connected to me," adds Kosovske, who is now a student rabbi at Congregation Shir Ami in Castro Valley. "I wanted some kind of proof to myself that what I was going through was a real spiritual struggle, that it wasn't some little phase. . . .

"Marking that permanently spoke to me. When the pain goes away, you have something beautiful," she says.

Beautiful, yes, but at the same time, because she is training to be a rabbi, there is a part of her that is ambivalent about it. "There are many things in the Torah that I don't agree with 100 percent or don't fit with me," she says. "You really have to check in with yourself and check in with God."

—Shoshana Hebshi, "Tattooed Jews—Despite Prohibitions and Censure, Some Wear Jewish Symbols as Badges of Their Identity," *J.: The Jewish News Weekly of Northern California*, January 16, 2004, www.jewishsf.com/content/2–0-/module/displaystory/story_id/21248/edition_id/434/format/html/displaystory.html (accessed June 23, 2006).

Source 3

In the great Talmudic tradition of her people, Ori Scherr scoured the literature, parsed the commentaries, and then, with her resolve firmly in place and her argument tightly constructed, dropped the T word on her parents.

Her father, a cantor at a Natick synagogue, shook his head. It's prohibited in the Bible, he told her. It will prevent you from being buried in a Jewish cemetery. It's an affront to victims of the Holocaust.

Her mother cut to the chase: Nice Jewish girls don't get tattoos.

Scherr, then an 18-year-old senior at Dover-Sherborn Regional High School, pondered her parents' advice and, in the equally time-honored tradition of adolescence, ignored it. The Aztec sun sign she had inked into her back is, to her way of thinking, as Jewish as the Star of David. In Hebrew, "Ori" means sun, and though she covers the tattoo when she attends synagogue, out of respect, she says the symbol is a fitting reflection of her Jewish identity.

Scherr is far from alone. In less time than it has taken Madonna to move from pop-star exhibitionist to tattooed Kabbalist, the 3,000-year-old Jewish taboo against body art has crumbled among some Jewish young adults. Thumb through the portfolio of almost any tattoo artist—there are now a half-dozen in the city—and you'll find traditional Jewish symbols of life and luck alongside menorahs and Hebrew blessings.

> —Douglas Belkin, "Jews with Tattoos: What if You Wanted a Tattoo, but Your Religion Prohibited It?" *The Boston Globe Magazine,* August 15, 2004, www.boston.com/news/globe/magazine/articles/2004/08/15/jews_ with_tattoos/?p1=email_to_a_friend (accessed June 23, 2006).

Source 4

And because, according to area funeral home directors, tattooed Jews aren't barred from Jewish cemeteries, the one cultural prohibition that does give pause to young Jews is the memory of Auschwitz, where Nazis had numbers tattooed on prisoners. But even this has been subject to reinterpretation.

"It's the opposite of a sacrilege," says Dan Jaye of Brighton, a rugged 23-year-old Jewish Marine veteran with the word "perseverance" tattooed in Hebrew on his left arm. Far from disrespecting Auschwitz victims and survivors, he says his tattoo honors them. "It's a tribute."

At least one survivor sees the wisdom in Jaye's words. "To me it just means we can make our own decisions now," says Steven Ross, a 73-year-old tattooed Auschwitz survivor and a driving force behind the

Holocaust Memorial near Faneuil Hall. "In a few more years, there won't be any more survivors left," he says. Then, the only Jews with tattoos will be the ones who asked for them.

—Douglas Belkin, "Jews with Tattoos: What if You Wanted a Tattoo, but Your Religion Prohibited It?" *The Boston Globe Magazine,* August 15, 2004, www.boston.com/news/globe/magazine/articles/2004/08/15/jews with tattoos/?p1=email_to_a_friend (accessed June 23, 2006).

Source 5

Jewish law forbids tattooing: Thou shall not make in thy flesh a scratch over the soul. But what if the Ta'un'uuans are right, and the soul is breath? Then aren't the scratches left on my soul by my needles really just the moments when my breath caught, my voice cracked, unable to find song?

—Jill Ciment, *The Tattoo Artist* (New York: Pantheon Books, 2005), 9.

Source 6

The American tattoo has changed enormously in the last thirty years. What started out as a highly standardized image commemorating patriotism, loved ones, or memorable events (an image that had not changed appreciably since the nineteenth century) quickly became linked to new social formations in the years following the end of World War II. Bikers and Chicano gangs began to shape the tattoo to their own lifestyles and aesthetics, changing the style, imagery, and set of meanings associated with the tattoo. Later, middle-class men and women also began to re-work the traditional images of the tattoo in order to fit their own changing lifestyles. Just as there is no single working-class tattoo (classic American tattoos, biker tattoos, and Chicano tattoos are easily distinguished from one another and occupy very different social positions), there is also no single middle-class tattoo. Since the eighties, tattoo styles have multiplied, and customers today can choose from tribal, neo-tribal, circuitry, Celtic, Japanese, neo-traditional, photo-realistic, Chicano-style, and a host of other styles and techniques. Images range from rain forest scenes, science fiction/fantasy scenes, portraits, copies of "fine art," children's drawings, Northwest Indian designs, and Sanskrit lettering, as well as the more traditional animals, flowers, and hearts. Along with the new images, tattoo clients can also choose from a selection of ideologies with which to make sense of their new tattoos. Tattoos can now represent spirituality, a connection to the earth, an instinctive drive, or a connection to the primitive. What makes these most recent transformations especially remarkable is that they have occurred within the span of about fifteen years.

—Margo DeMello, *Bodies of Inscription: A Cultural History of the Modern Tattoo Community* (Durham & London: Duke University Press, 2000), 189–190.

Third Case Study: High-Risk Behavior

David is 26. He has a strong sense of adventure. Coming from a family in which his parents were rather restrictive and repressive, he now wants to make up for lost time. He is not in a romantic relationship. He and his friends enjoy weekend outings in which they challenge one another to do new and increasingly risky things, such as:

a. Bungee jumping

b. Whitewater kayaking in remote places

c. Sky diving

d. Rock climbing

e. Drinking alcohol to excess

Although he sometimes feels that his friends have pushed him beyond a comfortable level of risk, so far he has always let peer pressure win out.

Questions

1. Assuming that David is not financially responsible to care for anyone else, what obligations does he have to protect his own life? If he has such duties, where do they come from and to whom do they apply?

2. How should he determine the levels of risk that are reasonable in deciding which activities he may properly do in life? After all, statistically the most dangerous place to be is within a mile of your own house, but that clearly should not deter David from going home!

3. Would your assessment of David's rights and responsibilities change if David had a life-threatening illness that impelled him to want to make the most of the years he had left?

Traditional Sources

[Note to readers: Refer also to "Traditional Jewish Sources Relevant to All Cases Studies," on page 3.]

On Alcohol and Drunkenness

1. Genesis 19:30–35

Lot went up from Zoar and settled in the hill country with his two daughters, for he was afraid to dwell in Zoar; and he and his two daughters lived in a cave.

And the older one said to the younger, "Our father is old, and there is not a man on earth to consort in the way of all the world.

Come, let us make our father drink wine, and let us lie with him, that we maintain life through our father."

That night they made their father drink wine, and the older one went in and lay with her father; he did not know when she lay down or when she rose.

The next day the older one said to the younger, "See, I lay with Father last night; let us make him drink wine tonight also, and you go lie with him, that we maintain life through our father."

That night also they made their father drink wine, and the younger one went and lay with him; he did not know when she lay down or when she rose.

2. Proverbs 20:1

Wine is a scoffer, strong drink a brawler; He who is muddled by them will not grow wise.

3. Proverbs 31:6–7

Give strong drink to the hapless
And wine to the embittered.
Let them drink and forget their poverty,
And put their troubles out of mind.

4. Ecclesiastes 10:19

They [ministers of the king] make a banquet for revelry, wine makes life merry, and money answers every need.

5. Babylonian Talmud Pesachim 113b

There are three whom the Blessed Holy One loves: One who does not get angry, one who does not get drunk, and one who does not insist on his due measure.

6. Babylonian Talmud Bava Batra 12b

Rabbi Huna ben Rabbi Yehoshua said, "He who is accustomed to drink wine, even though his heart is shut like a virgin, wine will open it . . . "

7. Babylonian Talmud Gittin 70a

Eight things are harmful in large quantities but beneficial in small ones: travel and sexual intercourse, riches and trade, wine and sleep, hot baths and bloodletting.

8. Babylonian Talmud Megillah 7b

Rava said: One is obligated to become intoxicated on Purim until one does not know the difference between cursed Haman and blessed Mordechai.

Rabbah and Rabbi Zera had a Purim feast together. They became intoxicated. Rabbah arose and slew Rabbi Zera. The next day Rabbah prayed for mercy and revived him. The following year [Rabbah] asked him [Rabbi Zera]: "Let master come and we will have the Purim feast together [again]". Rabbi Zera answered him: "Not every time does a miracle occur!"

9. *Sefer Kol Bo,* Laws of Megillah and Purim 45

And one is obligated to become intoxicated on Purim: One should not get drunk, for inebriation is forbidden completely. There is no greater sin than this, for it causes forbidden sexual relationships, murder, and many other sins. However, one should drink a little more than usual in order to increase happiness and also to create happiness and comfort the poor.

10. Shulchan Arukh, Orah Hayyim 695:2

One is obligated to get drunk on Purim until one does not know the difference between "Cursed is Haman" and "Blessed is Mordechai."

Gloss: And there are those who say that one need not get too inebriated; rather, drink a little more than usual and sleep, for during sleep one is unable to make the distinction [between "Cursed is Haman" and "Blessed is Mordechai"]. And whether one drinks heavily or a small amount, [it should be] with the intention to fulfill God's will.

On Taking Other Risks

11. Babylonian Talmud Pesachim 112a

Our masters taught: A man should not drink water from rivers or pools at night. If he drinks, his blood is on his own head, so great is the danger.

12. Jerusalem Talmud Berachot 4:4 [8b]

In all journeys, there is the presumption of mortal danger.

13. Babylonian Talmud Yoma 21a

He who sets out on a journey before cockcrow—his blood is on his own head.

14. Jerusalem Talmud Berachot 3:4 [6c]

R. Yose ben Halafta entered an alley, his ass driver behind him. When they reached a ditch with water in it, the driver said, "I would like to bathe." R. Yose said: "Do not court danger." The driver replied: "I wish to wash off my uncleanness." R. Yose repeated: "Nevertheless, do not court danger." When the driver still refused to heed him, R. Yose said, "He will go down and is not likely to come up again." Indeed, this is what happened.

15. Babylonian Talmud Shabbat 32a and Ta'anit 20b

R. Yannai said: "A man should never stand in a place of danger in the expectation that a miracle will be wrought in his behalf. Perhaps it will not be wrought, or if it is wrought, his merits will be diminished as a result." What is the proof? R. Hanin's interpretation of "I am unworthy of all the kindness that you have so steadfastly shown Your servant" (Genesis 32:11) as meaning that Jacob said to the Holy One: "I fear that because of the miracle You will perform for me, You will diminish my merits, so that, as a result of all the kindnesses so steadfastly shown me, I will come to be deemed quite unworthy."

16. Babylonian Talmud Pesahim 113a

Rav said to his son, Hiyya, "Do not take drugs [that create habits], do not take large jumps, do not have a tooth pulled. . . . "

17. Maimonides, *Mishneh Torah,* Laws of Ethics (De'ot) 3:1

A person may say, "Since jealousy, desire, honor, and similar things are a bad path and remove people from this world, I will separate myself from them and move away from them by doing the opposite." This person would not eat meat, not drink wine, not get married, not live in a nice home, not wear fine clothing; but rather, this person would wear sackcloth and uncomfortable wool and the like . . .

This is also a bad path down which one is forbidden to walk. The one who chooses this path is considered a sinner. . . .

Also, this category [of sinners] includes those who constantly fast. This is not a good path, for the Sages forbade us from afflicting ourselves with [constant] fasts.

18. Yehudah Ha-Levi, *The Kuzari,* Part 2, paragraph 50

The Divine law imposes no asceticism on us. It rather desires that we should keep the balance and grant every mental and physical faculty its due, without overburdening one faculty at the expense of another.

19. Yehudah Ha-Levi, *The Kuzari,* Part 3, paragraph 1

The servant of God does not withdraw himself from secular contact lest he be a burden to the world and the world to him. He does not hate life, which is one of God's bounties granted to him. . . . On the contrary, he loves this world and a long life because they afford him opportunities of deserving the world to come: the more good he does, the greater his claim on the world to come.

20. Shulchan Arukh, Hoshen Mishpat 427:8

It is a positive commandment to be very careful and guard oneself from any life-threatening obstacle, as it is said, " . . . take utmost care and watch yourselves scrupulously" (Deut. 4:9).

Contemporary Sources

Source 1

The positive steps we are commanded to take to preserve life and health are accompanied by the demand that we avoid danger and injury. . . . We certainly may not injure ourselves intentionally, let alone kill ourselves. Jewish law goes further, though, prohibiting us also from endangering our health unnecessarily, and viewing such an act as worse than a ritual prohibition.

—Elliot N. Dorff, *Matters of Life and Death: A Jewish Approach to Modern Medical Ethics* (Philadelphia: The Jewish Publication Society, 1998), 249.

Source 2

In the past, men and women found God—and their particular spiritual expressions—in bushes that burned, valleys of shadows and dens of lions. Some communed with the divine on the peaks of mountains. Others had mystical encounters in prison cells. Itinerant rabbis and explorer priests followed their callings to remote shtetls and uncharted villages. Some found the fullest manifestation of their faith through solitude, hunger, or other forms of denial. Some even found it through death and martyrdom. I understand the impulse toward the edge. My own experience with spirituality has taken place not only in synagogues and through holy books, but in dogsleds, squad cars, and cyberspace. It has taken me to the tundra of Alaska and the steppes of Central Asia. Existential struggle, not equanimity, has been the impetus for my quest, a quest that has uncovered the divine image within me but also brought me face-to-face with my inner darkness and demons.

—Niles Elliot Goldstein, *God at the Edge: Searching for the Divine in Uncomfortable and Unexpected Places* (New York: Bell Tower, 2000), xiii.

Source 3

I interpret the young people's escape to drugs as coming from their driving desire to experience moments of exaltation. In my youth, growing up in a Jewish milieu, there was one thing that we did not have to look for and that was exaltation. Every moment is great, we were taught, every moment is unique. Every moment can do such great things.

—Abraham Joshua Heschel, "In Search of Exaltation," in *Moral Grandeur and Spiritual Audacity: Essays,* edited by Susannah Heschel (New York: Farrar, Straus, Giroux, 1996), 228.

Source 4

You aren't alive anywhere like you're alive at fight club. When it's you and one other guy under that one light in the middle of all those watching. Fight club isn't about winning or losing fights. Fight club isn't about words. You see a guy come to fight club for the first time, and his ass is a loaf of white bread. You see this same guy here six months later, and he looks carved out of wood. This guy trusts himself to handle anything. There's grunting and noise at fight club like at the gym, but fight club isn't about looking good. There's hysterical shouting in tongues like at church, and when you wake up Sunday afternoon you feel saved.

Chuck Palahniuk, *Fight Club* (New York: W.W. Norton & Company, 1996), 51.

Source 5

The greatest risk is the risk of riskless living.

—Stephen R. Covey, *The 8th Habit: From Effectiveness to Greatness* (New York: Free Press, 2004), 183.

Source 6

. . . the most extreme conditions require the most extreme response, and for some individuals, the call to that response is vitality itself. . . . The integrity and self-esteem gained from winning the battle against extremity are the richest treasures in my life.

—Diana Nyad [U.S. long-distance swimmer], *Other Shores* (New York, Random House, 1978), cited by *Columbia World of Quotations*, www.bartleby.com/66/ (accessed June 27, 2006).

PART II

&

SYMPOSIUM

Modern Jewish Views of the Body

"A Body of Laws": Traditional Texts Speak to Contemporary Problems
Abraham J. Twerski

E VER SINCE the epochal work of Darwin, there has been an ongoing and often heated debate of creation vs. evolution. The concept of a Creator is not within the scientific realm; hence the question of whence came the primordial energy that resulted in the Big Bang is unanswerable. It might seem that the advocates of each position, for all their zeal, are engaged in an essentially philosophical argument that is of little moment in actual life. The combination of hydrogen and oxygen produces water, which is the basis of life. Whether this combination of elements was designed by an intelligent being or was a chance occurrence seems to have little application in our everyday lives.

However, the philosophical issue has major implications in regard to one aspect of human behavior: the rights of a person to one's own body. The attitude of Torah Judaism is expressed in the following paragraph:

In struggling with biomedical ethics, it is important to recognize that man does not have a proprietary interest in either his life or his body. If one looks for a legal category in order to explain man's rights and obligations with regard to his life and his person, it would be quite accurate to say that human life is a bailment, that man is a bailee, and that the Creator is the bailor. God has created man and entrusted him with this precious treasure called human life. Life has been entrusted to man for guardianship and safekeeping. Man is required to reserve and to prolong that life until such time as God chooses to reclaim it. That does not mean that the charge may not be burdensome. It certainly does not mean that man, left to his own desires, to his own intelligence and his very human emotions might not often wish otherwise. Indeed, in situations that are unfortunately too frequent, it would be only human for a person to wish otherwise.[1]

---

1. J. David Bleich, "Care of the Terminally Ill," in *Jewish Values in Health and Medicine,* edited by Levi Meier (Lanham, MD: University Press of America, 1991), 146.

Absent the concept of Creator, the above is meaningless. Inasmuch as there is no one else who owns one's body, it would follow that everyone is the proprietor of one's own body and may do with it whatever one wishes. Should there be societal concerns on this issue, they can be dealt with by the courts and legislatures. Otherwise, the body is no different from any other possession. One may care for it and preserve it, or one may neglect and destroy it.

Given the Judaic belief in Creation, and that the Torah is the expression of God's will, the rights one has to one's own body are dictated by the Torah and, in Orthodox Judaism, by *halakhah*, the body of laws developed by Torah scholars throughout Jewish history, including the Talmud, the Shulchan Arukh (codified laws), and responsa.

The scriptural source for rules on the care of one's body is the scriptural verse in Genesis 9:2:"Your blood, which belongs to your souls, I will demand." Although this appears to prohibit suicide, the Talmud (Bava Kamma 90b) extends this to self-injury, also referring to the verses that consider a Nazirite to be sinful because he has inflicted deprivation (of wine) on himself. Another source is the biblical prohibition of wanton destruction of any object, based on the verse prohibiting destruction of a fruit-bearing tree (Deuteronomy 20:19). The specific prohibition of self-mutilation, "You shall not cut yourselves and you shall not make a bald spot between your eyes for a dead person" (Deuteronomy 14:1) refers to the pagan ritual of mourning. That the Torah requires a person to preserve one's health is further derived from the verse, "But you shall greatly beware for your souls" (Deuteronomy 4:15). Although there are differences of opinion in the Talmud, *halakhah* states that self-injury is forbidden and that caring for one's health is obligatory, although this may be of rabbinical rather than scriptural origin.

An additional prohibition of self-endangerment may be derived from the commandment requiring a person to make a fence around his roof to prevent someone from falling (Deuteronomy 22:8). Based on this verse, Maimonides writes, "Many things are forbidden by the Sages because they are dangerous to life. If one disregards any of these and says, 'If I want to put myself in danger, what concern is it to others?' or 'I am not particular about such things,' *disciplinary flogging is inflicted upon him.*" He then goes on to cite a number of practices that the Talmud considers dangerous (Hilkhot Rotze'ach 11:4).

Not only is one prohibited from endangering oneself, but this is even more stringent than ritual prohibitions. Rabbi Moses Isserles, in his glossary on the Shulchan Arukh (Yoreh De'ah 116:5), writes, "One should avoid all things that might lead to danger, because *a danger to life is stricter than a (ritual) prohibition.* One should be more concerned about a possible danger to life than a possible (ritual) prohibition."

Given this attitude, an immediate application of this is that cigarette smoking is forbidden by the Torah. There is no longer any question about the toxicity of cigarette smoking. It has been established that smoking is the leading cause of lung cancer and chronic obstructive lung disease. It is also a significant risk factor in coronary artery disease and cancer of the larynx. There are more fetal complications if the mother smokes during pregnancy. A number of authoritative rabbis have formally ruled that smoking constitutes a violation of Torah law.

Whereas mutilation of one's body is prohibited, surgery that is beneficial to one's health is not only permissible but is also required by *halakhah,* as indicated by Maimonides' statement that "Inasmuch as a healthy and whole body is the way of God, because it is impossible to understand or know anything about God if one is ill, therefore, a person must avoid things that are injurious to the body and follow practices that are healthy and wholesome." Where the surgery corrects a disease, it is obligatory. Rabbi Moshe Feinstein ruled that surgery for cosmetic purpose is permissible if there is adequate indication that it is of psychological value (Iggrot Moshe, Hoshen Mishpat 66).

Whereas surgery to treat a disease is permissible and obligatory, the question arises whether one may injure his body by donating an organ. If one has no rights over one's body, may one subject oneself to surgery to help another person? The ruling is that the Torah requirement to save another person's life overrides the restriction on injuring one's body.

Just as one has no unrestricted ownership over one's body during lifetime, neither does the body belong to anyone other than God after death. Is it, then, permissible to mutilate the body by doing an autopsy? Again, the Torah requirement to save another person's life overrides the restriction on injuring one's body. The prevailing opinion is that if it is believed that the findings of the autopsy may be immediately beneficial to a patient, it may be performed.

Reclaiming Dignity, Freedom, Health:
The Jewish Body in America
Miriyam Glazer

You fashioned me in my mother's womb.

I praise You,

for I am awesomely, wondrously made.
>   —*Psalms 139:13–14*

Is a nose with deviation such a crime against the nation?
>   —*"If a Girl Isn't Pretty" from* Funny Girl[1]

TOWARD THE end of Tillie Olsen's 1960 short story "Tell Me a Riddle," the dying Eva begins to sing the heroic songs of her Russian youth, songs rich with hope for the newly dawned twentieth century. Her anguished husband listens with pain and wonder: pain that, unbeknownst to him, his dying wife still harbored their once-shared but long unuttered youthful idealism; wonder that as young people they had managed to feel so fervently optimistic, despite the suffering that marked their lives. Though their world had been "dark, ignorant, terrible with hate and disease," though they had lived "in the midst of corruption, filth, treachery, degradation," still, he realizes, "How we believed!" How they had "believed so beautifully" that the new century would bring an enlightened humanity, a peaceful, free, "loftier race" of human beings!

For a moment the old man is stricken with despair: What the twentieth century had in fact wrought was inconceivable barbarity and violence. That thought, though, is interrupted by another, as he suddenly pictures his and Eva's grandchildren in his mind's eye. For these children of America were youngsters

> whose childhoods were childish, who had never hungered, who lived unravaged by disease in warm houses of many rooms, had all the school for which they cared, could walk on any street, stood a head

---

1. Quoted by Felicia Herman, "The Way She *Really* Is: Images of Jews and Women in the Films of Barbra Streisand," in *Talking Back: Images of Jewish Women in American Popular Culture,* edited by Joyce Antler (Hanover, Mass.: Brandeis University Press, 1998), 173.

taller than their grandparents, towered above—beautiful skins, straight backs, clear straightforward eyes. "Yes, you in Olshana," he said to the town of sixty years ago, "they would be nobility to you." And was this not the dream then, come true in ways undreamed? he asked.[2]

Jews who *could walk on any street,* Jews with *beautiful skins, straight backs, clear straightforward eyes:* Can we contemporary American Jews even begin to fathom how magnificent, even miraculous, those phenomena could have seemed to him? To "walk on any street" means we are free; to have "beautiful skin" means we are healthy; to have a "straight back" means we have dignity; to have "clear straightforward eyes" means we are unafraid. From the point of view of Olsen's aged Jewish immigrant, the very bodies of these young Jews of America emanated a hitherto unfathomable sense of well-being, a confident sense of self, an at-homeness in the world: a "dream come true in ways undreamed."

But how foreign such a celebration of the Jewish body would have seemed to those very same Jews, the young men and women born in America! What the grandfather saw as "beautiful skin" they might have castigated as too oily; too acne prone; and maybe even too olive, too dark as well. The "clear straightforward eyes" probably needed glasses. And health? Well, what about allergies?

Particularly from the post-World War II era on, feeling free of the oppressive ills of the ghettos, shtetls, and fetid tenements of the past scarcely served as the measure by which American-born Jews experienced and envisioned their own bodies. The new generations compared their bodies not to the Jewish bodies of the Old World, but rather to the body types most favored, most idealized, by the gentile-dominated American culture of their own time and place. What comfort was it for a Jewish twenty-something man to know—as the anthropologist Franz Boas had demonstrated early in the century—that the children of immigrants tended to be taller than their parents, if, compared to WASP Americans, he felt too short? In the 1950s, when a Jewish teenager came upon the Charles Atlas ad at the back of a comic book, did he feel more like the skinny guy who gets sand kicked in his eyes, or the broad-chested bully who did the kicking? Like what Atlas's ad called the "runt" or, like Atlas promised,

---

2. Tillie Olsen, "Tell Me a Riddle," in *Jewish American Short Stories,* edited by Irving Howe (New York: Signet, 1977), 82–117.

the "Hero of the beach"? Did Jewish women fantasize about becoming television's maternal, Yiddish-inflected homemaker Molly Goldberg or the coolly serene, soon-to-be-princess-of-fairy-tale-Monaco Grace Kelly? Which of them looked more like a Barbie doll?

After all, how we *see* and how we *experience* our bodies are cultural constructions; the lenses through which we see ourselves and how we feel about what we see arc shaped by the culture we have internalized. As the writer Albert Memmi pointed out decades ago in *Portrait of a Jew:* "Generally speaking, I admit that I see my body in a certain way. I watch over it, I ask it certain questions, I apprehend certain replies from it. But . . . it is not because my body is what it is, but because I have a certain picture of my body, estranged, burdened with a culture. . . ."[3] The estrangement that Memmi describes is *caused* by the body's carrying the burden of a culture—a culture that denigrates Jews. As one North American Jewish woman reported to scholar Nora Gold:

> I have a girlfriend, she said to me once, "You have a gentile body," and I said, "What's a gentile body?" "Well, Jewish women have the hips and the this and the that. You have beautiful long legs, and small hips." When people say to me, "You don't look Jewish," it's a compliment . . . I take it as a compliment.[4]

A hundred and fifty years after Europeans categorized Jews by their noses, the legacy lives on: *Not even one* of the 47 women Gold interviewed liked her own nose. The Jewish attempt to be fully accepted by German society, wrote the mid 19th-century writer Moses Hess, would always be thwarted, because in the end the Germans did not object to anything the Jews believed; they objected to the Jews' "peculiar noses." Jews have long internalized that message. In the late 19th century, it was the son of a rabbi, Dr. Jacques Joseph, who began redesigning the Jewish noses of Berlin, even offering to do so free for the Jewish poor. In the 1970s, America's suburban Jewish girls got their "designer noses" before their bat mitzvah. In Gold's study, three of the women, as young girls, had "tried to force their noses into a more desirable, Aryan shape by holding them up or pressing objects against them."

---

3. Albert Memmi, *Portrait of a Jew* (New York: Viking Press, 1962), 118.
4. Nora Gold, "Canadian Jewish Women and Their Experiences of Antisemitism and Sexism," in *Celebrating the Lives of Jewish Women: Patterns in a Feminist Sampler,* edited by Rachel Josefowitz Siegel and Ellen Cole (Binghamton, NY: Haworth Press, 1997), 279–289.

Moses Hess could not imagine that Jewish noses, as distinct from Jewish religious practice, could be "reformed."[5] A little over a century later, in 1996, among the representations featured in the controversial "Too Jewish?" exhibit, by the Jewish Museum of New York, were Jewish princess tiaras, Barbie dolls, name changes, hair straightenings, casts of Jewish noses—and a whole series of drawings of nose jobs. Could not be "reformed" indeed!

The moment that Abraham Cahan's "Yekl" stepped off the boat at Ellis Island, renamed himself "Jake," and cut off his beard and side curls, the Americanization of the Jewish body began en masse. Since that time, the Jewish body has been less about Jews feeling at home in America than about *trying* to feel at home. Catapulted into the middle class and into the life of suburbia, we have either wished to remake our bodies or actually remade them to conform to the image valued by the dominant culture. But just as we were doing so, the very meaning of "home" and the innermost nature as well as the outer image of the American body were also changing—with profound and ever more troubling consequences for the American body today.

Media-driven and saturated with advertising, 21st century American culture is one of manipulative images, digitally created virtual reality. By now, the predigital world of the last century seems almost quaint. Yet it was that post–World War II industrial world that vastly proliferated and intensified the consumerism that shapes every aspect of our being today. First television helped to destroy family dinnertime, as the movie *Avalon* so vividly suggested, and then the food industry destroyed family dinner. Our diets underwent a radical alteration, changing our very capacity to feel. "Rapturously envisioning a day when virtually all contact between the cook and the raw makings of dinner would be obsolete," author Laura Shapiro has written, the food industry found that to process foods meant restricting their qualities of sensation. Manufactured foods could be only "very sweet, very salty, or very bland,"[6] meaning that the more we ate them, the more these eagerly advertised pseudo-foods numbed the American palate.

---

5. Quoted by Jay Geller, "(G)nos(e)ology: The Cultural Construction of the Other," in *People of the Body,* edited by Howard Eilberg-Schwartz (Albany: SUNY Press, 1992), 249.
6. Laura Shapiro, *Something from the Oven: Reinventing Dinner in 1950s America* (New York: Penguin Books, 2004), xvi–xvii.

"Strawberry" Jell-O? Our taste buds grew accustomed to artificial flavors. Most of the flavor of food comes from its aroma, so our sense of smell was also affected. Theoretically able to discern 10,000 different fragrances, our sense of smell began closing down—how else could anyone accept that a bathroom spray had a "fresh country scent"? Today, a disturbing 90 percent of the money the United States spends on food goes into processed food. This industrialization of the nourishment we take into our bodies, nourishment meant to energize our cells and keep our hearts beating and our minds thinking, has profound and pervasive consequences. It means our loss of the possibility of authentic sensory experience, of rich sensory memories, and, crucially, of a deeper apprehension of our lives.

Compare, for example, the experience of French-Jewish writer Marcel Proust (1871–1922). By just sipping a cup of tea soaked with a piece of madeleine, he was cast into the memories of his aunt, her home, and the town she lived in—with its people, houses, garden, and surroundings. Had he lived in our visually dominated culture, the memory would never have been evoked. Only seeing the madeleine could never have unleashed such an exquisite panorama. As Proust said in his *Swann's Way:* "When nothing subsists of an old past . . . smell and taste still remain for a long time, like souls . . . bearing . . . the immense edifice of memory."[7] In response to the psalmist's line, "Let every breath praise the Lord," the ancient rabbis asked, "And what does breath enjoy? A fragrant aroma" (Babylonian Talmud, *Berachot* 43b). But what "fragrant aroma" does packaged, processed food possess? What wells of intimate association does a manufactured, microwaveable, chemical-ridden meal evoke? How does it nourish the soul? The late Marlene Adler Marks vividly captured the synesthetic pleasures involved in experiencing Proust's "immense edifice of memory" in the preparation of traditional Jewish foods:

> I love making challah. I like the way it mixes the holy with the mundane. I like the way the dough, elastic but not too wet, reminds me of a powdered baby's bottom. . . . I like shaping the mound and punching down into its womb, and the dark oaky smell ripe with leaven and hope.

> Some years ago, seeming out of the blue, I started making gefilte fish. . . . I needed a different kind of connection to Passover, a connection beyond intellect.

---

7. Marcel Proust, *Swann's Way*, translated by Lydia Davis (New York: Penguin, 2002), 47.

Just as you're wondering why you're going through this sweaty ordeal, the magic begins. You feel the imaginary babushka on your head tying back your imaginary long dark hair. The walls of your American adobe home are replaced by the brick walls of the European ghetto, and up on the roof you hear Isaac Stern and his violin. That night, everyone at your table will marvel how you, a modern career woman, have miraculously turned into a gefilte-fish maker of the 19th century. . . . Your friends will smile. You will smile. Life will be a dream.[8]

For most of us, the visual sense has come to so dominate all of our other senses—of taste, of smell, of hearing, of touch—that those senses are nearly nullified. We are estranged from the palpable, the actual, the flesh-and-blood real—that is, from the experience of our own feeling selves, what the psychologist Alexander Lowen calls "the reality of the life of the body":

An overemphasis upon the role of the image blinds us to the reality of the life of the body and its feelings. It is the body that melts with love, freezes with fear, trembles in anger, and reaches for warmth and contact. Apart from the body, these words are poetic images. Experienced in the body, they have a reality that gives meaning to existence. Based on the reality of bodily feeling, an identity has substance and structure. Abstracted from this reality, identity is a social artifact, a skeleton without flesh.[9]

There's a prescient eeriness about Lowen's description of identity based on the image becoming only a "a social artifact, a skeleton without flesh." For his words capture the essence of the epidemic of eating disorders, particularly anorexia, besetting contemporary America. With thinness—often what one researcher called "impossible thinness"[10]—increasingly promoted by television commercials and programs, female models becoming thinner, and women's magazines relentlessly blaring on their covers diets that will make you "more attractive," 80 percent of women in American culture, one expert suggested, "wake up with body loathing." And girls as

8. Marlene Adler Marks, *A Woman's Voice* (Malibu, Calif.: On the Way Press, 1998), 154, 135.
9. Alexander Lowen, *The Betrayal of the Body* (New York: Macmillan, 1967), 5–6.
10. D. Hargreaves, "Adolescent Body Image Suffers from Media Images of the Impossibly Thin," *Flinders University Journal* 13, no. 9, (June 10–23, 2002).

young as eight, "bombarded by messages that tell them that appearance defines their identity," are already on diets.[11]

The other extreme is also true: 30-year-old Abigail of Case Study 1 is scarcely alone with respect to her problem with obesity. Obesity, too, has become an epidemic, threatening the health of millions of Americans, including a growing number of children. Predictably, researchers link American obesity to the growth of the fast-food industry, that mass marketing of the "very sweet, very salty, or very bland," and to hours of watching television. It is as though if you were unable starve yourself till you look like the anorexic model idealized on the screen, you might as well eat yourself into oblivion. To starve yourself is like a cry of the body desperate to ward off ingesting our culture's obsession with consumption; to destroy yourself with gluttonous passivity is like surrendering your very life to its power. In both cases, the culture devours you.

There is a very different way to be in the world. It is a way that can strengthen us to ward off the bombardment of messages from our image-obsessed and consumerist culture. It is a way that offers us a vital alternative, a radically different set of values from those of the dominant culture, one that urges us to honor and to cherish our body, to reawaken our dulled senses. It is a way that has the power to temper the influence of the commercial world on our sensibilities by deepening our sense of true connectedness with our innermost selves, with the cycles of nature, with history, and, vitally, with community.

It is not surprising that studies have shown that Jews who rejoice in their Judaism are relatively unlikely to suffer the kinds of body-image problems that beset those whose ache is for assimilation.[12] For Judaism teaches us that our bodies do not exist to serve commerce, nor do they function as mere vehicles of consumption or as objects to be critically assessed in light of the latest media-generated image of "in." Rather, in Judaism, human bodies are templates of holiness, evidence of God, and thus to be cared for and cherished. Indeed, the tradition regards even the

---

11. According to Catherine Steiner-Adair of the Harvard Eating Disorders Center. See Leni Reiss and Nadine Bonner, "Being Jewish in a Barbie World: Body-Image Negativism Poses Physical, Mental Threats to Men and Women," *Jewish News of Greater Phoenix,* November 6, 1998.
12. Aviva Cantor, *Jewish Women/Jewish Men: The Legacy of Patriarchy in Jewish Life* (San Francisco: Harper, 1992).

performance of our most basic bodily functions as an occasion to bless God for fashioning us with divine wisdom.

The Jewish tradition can offer us an opportunity to sensitize our own senses by rousing our awareness of the sheer miracle of nature's gifts. Every fruit, every vegetable, every loaf of bread is perceived as a gift of the Divine. Every time we smell fragrant herbs or spices; every time we enjoy trees, fruits, or oils; every time we sit down to eat or finish eating— all these are occasions for praising God as the creator of all things. The annual cycle of festivals reconnects us with rhythms of the seasons, with history, and with each other. Above all, the gift of the Sabbath urges us to live in a way that sets one day aside every week free from the "getting and spending" that lays waste our true powers, one day on which joyfully to experience our fundamental spiritual freedom.

The profound challenge we all face today is that of taking our place in the world while also internalizing the radical implications of this tradition, recognizing that it *is* a truly alternative pathway for experiencing ourselves and others, and giving ourselves a chance to be open to its gifts. If we do have the courage to remove the blinders that many of us live with and to take the first step, we just may discover that we are on the way to reclaiming the dignity, health, and sense of freedom the immigrant grandfather once beheld in his American-born grandchildren. And perhaps not too long after that we will wake up one morning with wondrous, unshakeable, awe—aware, like the psalmist, that we are "awesomely, wondrously, made."

Bodies on Loan: The Ethics of "Renting" a Body
Adam Goodkind

THE HUMAN body is, if nothing else, a funny thing. It is, for most of us, oddly shaped; and for everybody, it does odd things at odd times. Our body is, by definition, *ours,* and yet it still confounds us. During puberty, it seems that our bodies are completely out of our control, and that some malevolent creature, bent on the single objective of consistently embarrassing us, is at the helm. Our bodies boggle us when we work incessantly to improve our physique, to no avail, while seemingly everyone else we know maintains a seamless figure with little to no effort. As I grow older, I imagine my body will continue to confound me, as tasks that are effortless now become laborious and strenuous. What is amazing about this is that, 40 years from now, it will still be *my* body, but at the same time it will be a completely different body.

Perhaps it is the following paradox that confounds us: If our bodies are ours for our entire lifetime, why is it that they nevertheless feel completely separate from us? When we ponder how to treat our own bodies, there seem to be two equally compelling motivations. On the one hand, it seems that our bodies are exactly that, *ours.* Therefore, just as we can do what we like with *our* car or with *our* clothes, we should be free to do what we please with *our* bodies. On the other hand, tugging in the opposite direction is an equal and opposable force, à la Newton's third law of motion. This force tells us that somehow, for some reason, our bodies are not wholly ours. After all, something over which we have complete ownership implies that it is something over which we have complete control. As indicated earlier, this is something that everyone knows is not completely true when it comes to the body.

While it is not in vogue for college students today to quote Scripture, and especially not in vogue to quote from commentary on Scripture, I think a great deal can be gleaned from some of the messages found in these books. It does not matter whether you are observant or pious; the lessons are still equally valuable. I do not consider myself to be an observant Jew; nevertheless, the lessons one can learn from some of the parables transcend the question of whether or not you eat a Big Mac on Saturday afternoons.

A story is related to us in the Midrash Mishle, chapter 31, in which Rabbi Meir's children die while he is out studying on Shabbat afternoon. His wife is at home, and since she cannot bury her children on Shabbat, she puts a sheet over their bodies and waits for her husband to return. When Rabbi Meir returns, his wife asks him the seemingly innocuous question, "A while ago a man came and gave me a deposit. Now this man has come to reclaim it. Should we give it back to him?" Rabbi Meir responds that of course it should be returned, without question. At this point his wife takes him to the bedroom and reveals the two dead sons. Rabbi Meir is obviously stricken with grief; and in his despair, his wife reminds him of his answer to the previous question. At once he understands and recites a line from Job 1:21, "The Lord has given, and the Lord has taken away."

Whether or not one actually believes that the body is a gift from God is in truth irrelevant. Perhaps more truthful is the notion from Genesis 3:19, "For dust you are, and to dust you shall return." The bottom line, regardless of which one seems more plausible, is that our bodies are not wholly ours; they are, in a very real sense, on loan.

In this day and age, we often do not like to think of our bodies as the property of someone or something else. Our laws, and in fact our very Constitution, are based on the premise of autonomy. We are free to pursue our desires and free to express ourselves as we choose. Therefore, the idea of something less than full autonomy seems to be reminiscent of medieval times, when most people were serfs, serving under the restrictions of their lords.

As a child of the postmodern age (or whatever the philosophy *du jour* is), we seem beholden to the idea that education is freedom from tutelage (cf. Kant) and that religion is for the most part a sham. What has amazed me though, over and over again, is that no matter how much I believe these two ideas, the sheer commonsense benefits of taking care of one's body supersede any doubt I may have in a Creator, and the wisdom of the past cannot be defeated merely by doubting its motivations.

Being part of the "anything goes" generation, I completely understand the idea of doing anything you want with your body. I have at many times sought to push my body to its limits to explore what it can and cannot do. Let's look at three different scenarios, which each in its own way has something to say about how we should treat our bodies: body piercing, skydiving, and prosthetics. And no, they are not as esoteric or unrelated as they may initially appear. Further, I think if we keep in mind the idea

41

that the body is a rental, and not property that we own, then a lot of the decisions will naturally fall into place.

Let's look first at the practice of piercing. The practice is commonplace today, certainly for females and even, to a lesser degree, for males as well. In fact, after I was accepted into college, I pierced my ear cartilage as a congratulatory gift to myself, and my (relatively socially conservative) parents did not mind too much. The Law Committee, which makes halakhic (legal) decisions for the Conservative Movement, wrote an interesting decision (called a *teshuvah,* "a responsum") concerning both tattooing and body piercing (www.rabbinicalassembly.org). The bottom line was that body piercing is acceptable, while tattooing is not. This decision was primarily based on various passages from the Bible, some of which condemned marking the flesh, and others of which permitted piercing.

What I find most interesting about this decision, however, is how it reflects on the idea of renting the body. It is irrelevant whether people believe they are renting their body from a higher power or from the earth. Rather, all that is necessary to think about is the fact that, undoubtedly, we are renting our bodies from our future selves. There is pretty much no way to deny this. If we start from this frame of reference, the decisions we make concerning our bodies become clearer. I think that even the most rebellious teenager knows that thirty years down the road, a giant tattoo on his or her forearm will look pretty ridiculous. A few dozen face-piercings will look equally ridiculous; however, piercings have the benefit of being reversible, so that rash decisions can be amended. Further, a big part of the aforementioned *teshuvah* focuses on respecting one's parents; in a very real way, our parents are our future selves. Thus this notion seems to make a great deal of sense. We should respect our parents not simply because they are our parents, but because they also provide insight that may seem out of touch but actually comes with pretty significant hindsight.

This seems to point to the idea that while much of Jewish law may seem antiquated today, there really is a great deal of sense behind it. Just because the Bible seems old and out of fashion to so many today, this does not make the ideas derived from it irrelevant. Following Jewish law is not necessarily predicated on belief in the same God in which the authors of the Talmud believed. Sometimes all that is required is common sense and a mind open to the notion that observance or belief does not necessarily imply simplemindedness.

Keeping this notion in mind, let's now take a look at how we might make a decision regarding skydiving. The issue that seems to come to the forefront here is not so much permanence. After all, the consequences of skydiving seem to be binary—you either fail and die or succeed and live. Therefore, the decision regarding skydiving seems to center more on safety and not body rental. After all, renting from a future nonexistent self seems to raise utterly unfathomable metaphysical issues.

What then, are the parameters that should be considered when deciding on whether or not to go skydiving? One of the factors that Jewish law always seems to take into account is risk versus benefit. It would seem, then, that skydiving would, without question, be off limits. However, is skydiving really that risky? Compared to sitting quietly in front of the television, the answer is yes, skydiving is risky. However, when skydiving with a trained professional and with a backup parachute, the risk is actually not very high. Most skydiving deaths are the result of trying daredevil maneuvers or complicated acrobatics.

In this way, the decision of whether or not to go skydiving actually has some parallels to the decision of whether to get a piercing. In the above-mentioned *teshuvah*, the author mentions the fact that it is essential for one to choose a piercer who uses sanitary instruments and upholds a high standard of safety. Getting a piercing from a shady, back-alley "piercing artist" is never permissible. Taking this into account, it seems that Jewish law says that some risk is permissible, but unnecessarily high risk is not. Although this may seem like splitting hairs, it also puts responsibility on the individual because one cannot just look in a book to make a decision. Rather, as a responsible Jew, one should ask whether or not the danger associated with an activity outweighs the enjoyment gained from this activity.

Part of being a good Jew is getting a maximum amount of enjoyment out of life. Most Jews today do not believe in an afterlife; and as a result, it is incumbent upon every Jew to enjoy this life, your only life, as much as possible. However, this is not a ticket to be reckless or irresponsible because there are still parameters within which we must act. Nevertheless, these parameters were not set up by a group of irrational rabbis whose decision making was dictated solely by an unshakable fear of God. Rather, these rabbis asked the question of how to make Jewish law work with everyday life. Thus these parameters were established according to common sense and make just as much sense today as when they were written down over 1,000 years ago and long before people were jumping out of airplanes.

Finally, we come to the notion of prosthetics. The logical connection from skydiving to prosthetics is not immediately obvious, but I think that it will become clear. Going back to the argument concerning skydiving, the central theme for one to keep in mind is safety. If done properly, skydiving is relatively safe, and thus the possible benefit outweighs the possible risk. I think that this is the most important criterion to keep in mind when thinking about prosthetics, or any sort of body alteration or enhancement.

Again though, I do not think it is a matter of simply evaluating "safety" in a vacuum but rather evaluating safety as compared to benefit. For this reason, while all prosthetics and body improvements have some sort of benefit, they should not all be treated equally. For instance, getting lip implants or lip augmentations has a certain amount of risk associated with the procedure. Although the risk is minimal, it still strikes me as an unnecessary risk. If we are viewing our bodies as something not wholly ours, then I think that getting a procedure such as this is being irresponsible and reckless.

However, let's also look at a very different type of body improvement. Let's say that someone lost a leg in a car accident or that her leg was severely injured beyond repair. Keeping the same criterion in mind— that is, risk versus benefit—I think we will come to a very different conclusion. Here it seems that the benefit of getting a prosthetic leg is an enormous benefit. Again, as with the lip surgery, there is an inherent risk involved in the surgery. However, because the benefit is so great, it far outweighs the risk of this situation.

One important facet of Judaism that many people overlook, however, is the importance of making things beautiful. While this may seem somewhat superficial, it is actually an important part of our religion. For instance, it says in Genesis 15:2, "This is my God and I shall glorify Him." The Rabbis who wrote the Mekhilta, a commentary on Exodus, understood this to mean that one should always perform the mitzvot with as much beauty as possible, as an act of devotion to God. Therefore, it is actually incumbent upon us to make things in our lives more beautiful. Again, however, I think that more important than beauty are the overall risks we take. Therefore, it seems that this should be of primary importance.

Looking back, it appears that three very different considerations have all pointed in relatively the same direction. Viewing our bodies as "rented" is not just a component of a dogmatic religion. Rather, by viewing our bodies in this manner, we will make decisions that will pay off in dividends farther down the road, much farther than anyone my age can really see.

While this may seem to go against the notion of unlocking all of our bodily potential, I think it is in fact just the opposite. Not all of our bodily potential can be unlocked through extreme sports or uncultivated experimentation. It may, and often does, seem this way during one's college years. However, I think that my body holds potential down the road that I cannot even fathom at this point. By acting within certain limits, I am allowing myself to experience these future experiences.

I realize, very fully, that following the commandments of Judaism is not often easy, nor do the commandments always make sense. However, the more thought I give to them, the more they seem to be pretty logical, and quite practical. Our bodies, as I noted earlier, are funny things. They push and pull us in opposite directions and make us do crazy things. They usually do not cooperate with us and very often do not look the way we want them to. However, I think that if we use some of the wisdom of our religion as a guide, we can help ourselves to live a much more fulfilling life. It does not require blind faith or adherence to dogmas. Rather, all that is required is an open mind and a little bit of common sense.

Men's Bodies, Women's Bodies

Reflections of an Athlete

Lenny Krayzelburg

From the Soviet Union to the United States

I WAS BORN in Odessa, which at that time was part of the Union of Soviet Socialist Republics but today is part of Ukraine. I began swimming lessons at age five and at age nine was chosen as one of 45 to be part of a group sponsored by the army to train for the Olympics. From six in the morning to six at night, we trained together in swimming, along with academics. It was very intense and very competitive. When I left Odessa at age 13, only 20 of the original group were left. I felt that I had to leave; but I also enjoyed the atmosphere of being with the group, bonding with them, and competing with them. We spent more time together than we spent with our families. At age 10 we lifted weights four days a week; you do not see that here. They were clearly trying to take us to the highest level in competitive sports, because there were two things that were important there—namely, we had to be better than the United States in both military activities and sports. Those were the goals that were set before us.

Athletics helped shape who I am as an individual. The great intensity and pressure of the swimming program in Russia developed my character; it taught me that accomplishing anything requires great effort and tenacity. Swimming, especially, demands that you set goals and then use your own personal dedication and perseverance to achieve them. That lesson carried over to my schoolwork, as well. I love history especially. But I always trace my determination back to athletics, where I learned that I am responsible for achieving my goals.

I feel that I have been privileged to have a talent to swim, and I think that every person has his or her own talents. People who are successful realize their talent, explore it, and make the best of it. Most people do not realize their talents. If you are fortunate to be really good at something, you should take advantage of that as long as you can, because it may not last forever. But it is hard to let go and move on. So even though I have had several shoulder surgeries and will probably not compete in the 2008 Olympics, every once in a while I think that I could possibly compete again.

Sports is not going to be forever. We all understand that. Certain professional athletes will make a lot of money, but even that will end. Your education, however, will always be with you, even when your body is no longer able to excel or even engage in sports.

First Case Study

I actually experienced something very close to this case. The swim school I established last July depends on customer service. When we opened, we got busy very quickly, and I needed another person for office work. There was a lady who came in to interview, and I thought that her skills would make her ideal for the job; but she was quite a bit overweight. I'm guilty of thinking the way the employer did in this case because I was not sure whether she would be the right fit for us. After all, we are associated with sports, and I did not know whether parents would enroll their children if their first contact with the school was with an overweight person. If we are promoting health, activity, and safety, it looks odd if one of our staff members is not taking care of herself physically. Maybe she was sick or had some other condition that did not allow her to lose weight, but I made a decision not to hire her.

As my company has grown, however, I now realize that hiring someone overweight does not matter. I really struggled to find another person for that job. Although other people who were more physically fit applied for the job, none of them knew how to connect with people as well as that lady did. It taught me a really good lesson; within a half a year I changed my view completely. In the end, I hired someone else who was quite a bit overweight because of how accommodating she is, how pleasant she is on the phone, how well she is able to help the parents, how she goes out of her way to make sure that the parents will leave happy. I have not heard any complaints about her from parents that concerned her weight.

That says a lot about not only how I see the body but how my customers conceive of bodily issues. In fact, I now have a swimming teacher who is also overweight, but I hired her because she connects really well with the children. Kids immediately feel close to her, and that helps her do a great job in teaching them to swim. I think that that is the bottom line. Everyone remembers his or her first swimming instructor because swimming is about safety in a new and dangerous medium. I want to make sure that I find people who are able to connect with children by creating a bond with them so that they trust the instructor to keep them safe. To me, it does not matter how they look; it is rather their ability to connect emotionally. In fact, I have hired a number of people who never taught swimming before. You can teach people how to teach swimming, especially with the procedures that we have developed. You cannot, though, teach people how to give the emotional support that the child needs from the adult; you either have it or you do not. When I hire staff, I look mostly for the ability to communicate emotional support because that will go a lot further than anything else in making children comfortable in the water. This is just a business decision; it is not based on larger values of fairness, although I feel bad about what I did with the first woman for moral as well as practical reasons.

Because I largely hire young adults, I am not as worried as some employers might be about the insurance and absentee problems that overweight employees might bring. Even so, I have established a structure to encourage good health. Specifically, in addition to their salary, we pay people a bonus for every hour that they work so that they strive to be here each day they are scheduled to be here. Again, we are in the business of creating bonds with children, and you do not want to change instructors with a three-year-old who is just learning how to swim. So that is an incentive for people not to miss work and indirectly for people to take care of themselves so that they will not need to be absent.

Second Case Study

I am not a big fan of tattoos, and in my opinion the degree to which people have themselves tattooed has gotten out of hand. I remember that when I came to this country, tattoos were not popular, and people who had them confined them to parts of the body that were not visible. Now it seems that every other teenager has some type of tattoo on any and all parts of the body.

Why am I opposed to tattoos? Because I think that your body is a very sacred thing. A tattoo might look okay when you are 20 or 21, but what is it going to look like when you are 55 or 60? A sagging body with the tattoos sagging on it is just not going to look good. So I think that most people who get tattoos are just living in the moment, without thinking about what is going to happen down the road; and I think that a person should consider the fact that what looks good on you today will probably not look good on you 30 or 35 years from now.

Are there reasons other than aesthetic ones for deciding not to be tattooed? Yes, if a person wants to become more seriously Jewish. So if

Chuck is studying Torah and changing his lifestyle accordingly, that is an important thing that he should consider. I think that if you are going to do something, you should do it all the way. So if he is going to become observant, he should have his tattoos removed, given that the Torah does not allow them, and he certainly should not add more.

Third Case Study

It is David's personal decision as to whether to protect his life. He needs to make those decisions on his own. It is not a good thing to drink alcohol to excess, especially repeatedly. But he has a right to enjoy today to the fullest because he does not know what will happen tomorrow.

If he were married, then he is not living for himself any more. So then his actions will affect his wife. It will add stress and make his wife worry if he engages in dangerous activities. Actually, now that I think about it, even while he is single, he has a duty to his parents not to affect their lives in a negative way. Obviously, losing a child is as bad as it can get for a parent.

Also, if David is really a free-wheeling guy, I do not think that he appreciates how few Jews there are in this world and therefore how precious every Jew is. With only 13 or 14 million Jews in the world, we are obligated to take care of ourselves and to help and support each other in any way we can.

Does that make us more than individuals who have the right to decide what we want to do in life? We do, in general, have the right to decide what we want to do in life, but we also need to be conscious of the fact that our actions can affect others in very positive or negative ways. The need to carry on our ongoing tradition also imposes duties on us to get married, to have children, and to support each other.

Even if David knows that he is going to die in a year, he might still have a positive effect on others. I love the poster that says "A hundred years from now it is not going to matter how big your bank account was. What is going to matter is whether you made a difference in a child's life." That is a perfect example of how he might make life worthwhile even in the time remaining to him.

On Judaism

Although my family did not practice anything Jewish, my last name made it clear to me and to everyone else in Odessa that I was Jewish. I do not think that I look Jewish, and so a person who saw me on the street would not know that I was Jewish. But a name like Krayzelburg made me stand out as a Jew. As a result, from time to time anti-Semitic slurs were directed my way.

My dad's grandfather was a rabbi; he was killed during World War II. But his commitment to Judaism did not carry on to my dad's father, my dad, or us. My mother's father was not Jewish. My mother's mom was, and so I am legally Jewish, even though only three of my four grandparents were Jewish. But my family did not do any specifically Jewish activities to strengthen our Jewish identity.

When we came to this country, I slowly learned about the Jewish holidays and traditions. Part of that was through the Jewish Community Center, when we attended a Purim carnival and the like. I never really made an effort to learn much about Jewish culture because there were so many other things that overwhelmed me in the process of getting accustomed to this country. But I did go to the Russian synagogue here on Yom Kippur. More important, I had a friend from Israel who was an observant Jew, but not an Orthodox one, and he taught me about Jewish traditions and took me to his Conservative synagogue. After the 2000 Olympics, I wanted to start studying Torah more seriously, but I put that aside to train for the 2004 Olympics. Still, one day I definitely want to read the Torah to understand it. That is definitely still my goal, and I know that I will make that happen. But I want to study with a rabbi. Since I have never studied it before, I need someone to help me make sense of it. Nevertheless, I do read history quite a bit.

I got a Tikkun Olam Award recently from the Jewish Federation. I have been doing many things with Jewish organizations. I have helped HIAS (Hebrew Immigrant Aid Society), the organization that sponsored us to come here. I am very involved with the Jewish Centers of America; I run swimming camps at Jewish Center camps around the country. I went to the Maccabiah games a couple of times. So I have been getting involved with Jewish children and Jewish organizations. I am on the Board of Tikvah, which builds schools and housing for Jewish children in Odessa who are orphans. The Jewish people in Odessa were able to earn a better living than non-Jews, and the people who run the big companies in Russia are largely Jews. That is why it is ironic that there are Jewish orphans in Odessa. Philanthropy did not exist in the Soviet Union because everything was sponsored by the government. The conditions may not have been ideal, but the government sponsored whatever there was. But now it is somewhat better.

I never got deep into what it means to be a Jew. I have been to Israel a couple of times, though. For me, I am most proud about how rich the Jewish tradition is and how Jews have managed to persevere through many hardships in so many times and places. In every period, Jews in large numbers were maimed or killed, and the millions that we lost in the Holocaust is mind-boggling to me. To know that I am a Jew as those people were is very special to me. Unfortunately, they struggled throughout their lives. But they were never ashamed of their Jewish identity; they were very proud of it. I appreciate that I was born a Jew so that I can carry on that heritage. I did not know that in Russia, but my eyes opened up to that when I came to this country.

I am married to a woman from Odessa whom I met in Brooklyn after being fixed up when I was there to do some work for HIAS. Her mother is Jewish but not her father. We have twin daughters who are eight months old. I want them to learn more about Judaism than I did; I intend to send them to Pressman Academy (a Conservative, Solomon Schechter day school).

Circumcisional Circumstances: Circumspecting the Jewish Male Body

Harry Brod

I HAVE A cartoon that in a simple line drawing depicts a bearded man in a simple cloak standing on a mountaintop, holding a staff and addressing a cloud hovering above him. The caption reads: "You mean you want us to cut the ends of our dicks off?"

I have been asked to address issues of the Jewish male body, so I may as well not beat around the burning bush but get right to the heart of the matter. If there is any single predominant issue of the Jewish male body, it has to be circumcision. To avoid it would be to ignore the proverbial elephant in the room.

That cartoon was sent to me years ago by my friend Michael Kimmel, who wrote a very fine article on the decision that he and Amy Aronson (married to each other and both Jewish) made not to circumcise their son (*Tikkun*, May/June 2001). In it, he tells a story of a close friend of his, a child of Holocaust survivors, who did have his son circumcised. That was *my* story, and my decision was based on a story my mother told me.

My mother was a German Jew who lost all of her immediate family in the Holocaust. She told me that her brother had been on his way to escape when he was halted by Nazi soldiers at the train station. They identified him as a Jew by forcing him to pull down his pants, and they executed him.

I found compelling the arguments against circumcision—namely, that it was an outmoded tradition that needlessly and unjustifiably inflicts pain on a helpless infant. But as I struggled over whether to circumcise my son, that story kept coming back to me. Despite the powerfully persuasive arguments against it, I was simply unable to leave my son uncircumcised. That felt to me like a betrayal of what my people had died for, including specifically my uncle, whom I never got to meet. My feelings ran much deeper than the level of rational argument. The power of the nonrational was forcefully brought home to me.

The invitation to write on the male Jewish body for this volume has brought me back to the issue of circumcision and compels me to rethink the reasons for it.

For many Jews, the circumcised penis is the defining mark of being a Jew. Theologically and legally speaking, this is simply an error, for Jewish identity is conferred by parentage or conversion, not by any sign on the body. Yet the idea that circumcision confers Jewish identity has a deep and powerful hold on many Jews, even those not otherwise particularly observant.

I am also asked to respond to the sources and cases provided here. None of these, however, directly addresses the issue of circumcision. So let us follow time-honored rabbinic tradition and ask whether any of these sources or cases embody principles that may be applied to the case of circumcision.

The first classic source is from Leviticus (19:28): "You shall not make gashes in your flesh for the dead, or incise any marks on yourselves: I am the LORD."

The first part of the passage is a source for cutting one's clothes rather than oneself as a sign of mourning. The second part gives me pause. Isn't circumcision incising a mark upon oneself and therefore prohibited? Surely there must be powerful reasons for this practice, in the face of what seems a clear commandment that human flesh should be left intact. What, then, are the reasons given for circumcision?

Our volume's sources and cases suggest that one common justification should really not be given great, or perhaps even any, weight. The boy should *look like* his father, many insist, and this is held to be extremely important for his development, especially for his Jewish identity. But it seems hard to justify cutting into and removing part of the flesh for the mere sake of appearance, given the principle of the sanctity of the intactness of the flesh suggested by the Leviticus passage and its application to the issue of tattooing. If being tattooed is such a serious transgression, then the injunction against defacing the body seems so strong that there must be more than aesthetic reasons for circumcision. Our texts suggest that such a reason for the practice is not only insufficient but probably illegitimate.

Our texts emphasize the importance of health considerations, often used to justify circumcision. This line of reasoning raises two problems. First, this does not get one to Jewish circumcision. These reasons lead only to the medical procedure; but when performed without accompanying Jewish rituals, this is profoundly unsatisfactory. Further complications arise because certain Orthodox practices raise their own medical problems in the contemporary world, requiring the *mohel* to suck blood from the wound orally, raising the possibility of disease transmission (some versions of this Orthodox rite avoid direct contact, for example, by sucking through a tube, but this is not universal).

Second, the medical evidence is far from clear, to say the least. Much if not most of the evidence suggests that circumcision offers no clear medical benefit. Most medical associations throughout the world, including in the United States, now no longer support routine circumcision. Claims that it helps to reduce the incidence of sexually transmitted diseases, infections, and penile cancer have generally not been validated by scientific studies. (The most notable exception is a very recent study of HIV/AIDS transmission.) Earlier views that the infant felt no pain during the procedure have been discredited.

If aesthetic and health considerations seem not to justify the practice, we are left with cultural and religious reasons. The problem is, there has never been agreement on precisely what these reasons are, and contradictory things are often said.

There is the purely traditionalist argument. We do it because we have always done it. The act has been hallowed through its passage from generation to generation. But the tradition itself has always asserted that meaning arises intrinsically in each ritual enactment, not merely as one link in a chain.

In the defining biblical text God says to Abraham:

> I will make you exceedingly fertile, and make nations of you. . . .
> Such shall be the covenant between Me and you and your offspring
> to follow, which you shall keep: every male among you shall be circumcised. You shall circumcise the flesh of your foreskin, and that
> shall be the sign of the covenant between Me and you. And throughout the generations, every male among you shall be circumcised at
> the age of eight days (Genesis 17: 6, 10–11).

In this text, circumcision is linked to fertility, as opposed to the Leviticus text, cited earlier, that links bodily incisions to death. One important, though not dominant, strand of ancient rabbinic interpretation saw God's commandment to circumcise as intended to symbolize God's own acts of creation, described in Genesis as acts of separation that establish clear demarcations, conferring form on formlessness. Circumcision's separation of the flesh is seen here as a symbolically re-creationist forming of the flesh.

The major strain of early rabbinic interpretation linked circumcision to blood sacrifice, emphasizing a different aspect of the procedure, focusing not on separating the foreskin from the penile shaft but on drawing blood in its removal. On this view, male genital bleeding, ritually enacted and controlled by men, is superior to female menstrual bleeding, occurring naturally and uncontrolled. The sacrifice of the foreskin is culture's triumph over nature, a view that leads toward the next interpretative strain.

In the further development of medieval Judaism, the meaning of circumcision changed from symbolic (of either creation and reproduction or sacrifice) to actual, as it came to be seen as desexualizing, elevating men above their animal nature and subjugating their sexual impulses to their will. For many Jews, whether they are aware of it or not, the teachings of Maimonides *are* what they understand as the teachings of Judaism. The view of Maimonides, the preeminent Jewish philosopher and court physician to the twelfth-century Egyptian Muslim Sultan Saladin, was extremely influential, as he celebrated the importance of circumcision because he believed it lessened sexual arousal and sensitivity in men.

To those of us familiar with modern intellectual traditions, this sounds very Freudian. We would interpret the reasoning that circumcision lessens male sexual urges as Judaism's wanting men to sublimate (i.e., to repress and redirect) their sexual urges into religious ones. Or we might say, with more recent Freudian theorist Jacques Lacan, that circumcision represents the literal embodiment of male patriarchal authority or, in Lacanian terms, the inscription of the phallus (i.e., the meaning we attach to masculinity) onto the penis (a mere bodily organ), marking the erection of patriarchy. In this theoretical tradition, circumcision is seen as both masculinizing and feminizing, the former because the ritual emphasizes the importance of the penis/phallus, and the latter for the seemingly opposite reason, because the cut is seen as deemphasizing the importance of the penis/phallus.[1]

It is in this concept of patriarchy that I believe we have reached the real meaning of circumcision. For circumcision is above all a male-to-male transmission of Jewish identity, one that dramatically centers Judaism on fathers and sons and marginalizes mothers and daughters. It therefore requires full and frank discussion.

---

1. These paragraphs above draw on my "Circumcision," in *International Encyclopedia of Men and Masculinities,* edited by M. Flood, J. K. Gardiner, B. Pease, and K. Pringle (London: Routledge, 2007), pp. 67–69.

Some may feel that this discussion has already been more frank than they would have liked and may have been made uncomfortable by such explicit discussion of penises. That is precisely the point. That which is undiscussed and hidden (or, in Freudian terms, unconscious) operates all the more powerfully precisely because of its hiddenness. The authority of men is reinforced by the taboo on discussing the specifics of the male body.

Judaism offers profound insights into the power of hiddenness. For we serve a hidden God, one with an unknowable name. When Moses asks of the Burning Bush what he shall answer when Pharaoh asks who sent him, God does not give Moses a name but instead responds with the cryptic formula *"Ayeh Asher Ayeh"* (I Am-Was-Will Be Who/What I Am-Was-Will Be).

Ancient mystical and magical traditions in play here, older than Judaism itself, teach that knowledge of a name confers power over what is named. (On one traditional interpretation in this vein, God calls upon Adam to name the animals as a sign of humanity's dominion over the creatures of the Earth, though this is not the only way to interpret the story, and ecologically sensitive Judaism offers differing interpretations.) Further, naming is by definition an act of separation—any name or definition works by establishing limits and boundaries, differentiating this from that. To name God would, therefore, be to limit God, contradicting Jewish teachings.

For Judaism, the privilege of namelessness or hiddenness is God's alone. To respect the distinction between the human and the divine is therefore to deny such hiddenness to humans. As humans are called upon to honor God's hiddenness, they are thereby called upon to reveal themselves.

To take to ourselves this privilege of hiddenness is thus to claim for ourselves an identity and authority that is God's alone. It is an almost idolatrous sort of arrogance, of hubris. But men do this all too frequently. They, and at this point I must in all honesty say "we," hide our selves, our deepest and most honest thoughts and feelings, even from our loved ones, because we understand or intuit that knowledge is power, and to expose ourselves is to give others potential power over us.

Men need to surrender this patriarchal power and its pretensions to near divinity in order to reclaim their humanity. Patriarchal power diminishes men as well as women, as patriarchal imperatives to hide our selves from others leads us to hide even from ourselves. We suffer from a peculiarly male malady that psychologists are beginning to call "alexithymia," an inability to attach words to emotions from the Greek and Latin: *a* (without), *lexus* (words), *thymos* (emotions). When asked how we are feeling, we are often unable to articulate a response. Problems that cannot be named cannot be solved, and so we stay locked inside our emotional straitjackets, suffering higher rates than women of heart attacks, ulcers, suicides, and early deaths because of the emotional pressures that necessarily remain unreleased because they remain unrevealed.

We have traveled far in this discussion of the Jewish male body. I have used our reluctance to discuss the penis, its hiddenness, as a metaphor for the hidden dimensions of the male soul, seeing in both the maintenance of patriarchal authority by cloaking masculinity in mystery. When I was asked to contribute to this volume on Jewish choices and voices regarding the body, I was not surprised to discover that the discussion had come to focus on women's bodies. But in this focus on women I find not the voice of feminism but rather the voice of patriarchy.

Our world is deeply gendered. The cultural dichotomy between mind and body corresponds to a dichotomy between the masculine and the feminine, with women coming to be seen as stupefied bodies—that is, sex objects, and men becoming disembodied intellects. Emphasizing the embodiedness of men therefore de-privileges rather than re-privileges men. It is egalitarianism, not exhibitionism.

Attention to the male body not only will help empower women, as it reveals the hiddenness of male privilege, but is in men's real human interests too. Seeing men as essentially minds rather than bodies creates role models of Jewish men as scholars rather than athletes. This is not to in any way diminish the value of the ideal of the Jewish scholar but rather to lament how Jewish men have not as fully developed the potential of their bodies, to our great loss.

I intend through this essay to challenge as patriarchal the practice of circumcision and, more broadly, our reluctance to discuss the secrets men keep and the rituals by which their power is kept and to call for their full and frank discussion. I do not presume to know what the results of that discussion should be. I do presume to know that we will be the better for having it.

I could and perhaps should end here, but I began with a personal perspective and feel called upon to end on one too. The decision to circumcise my son is behind me, so when I think about the issue now, it is in terms of the decision my children may be called upon to make. In my thoughts now it is not so much the story with which I began, but more a quote from British writer E. M. Forster, who wrote: "If I had to choose between betraying my country and betraying my friend, I hope I should have the guts to betray my country." Mindful of the pain of circumcision, for me this translates into: "If I had to choose between betraying my tradition and betraying my son, I hope I would have the guts to betray my tradition."

I wish for my children the courage to confront the question.

Circumcision: The Medical Imperative
Accompanying the Religious Imperative[1]

Samuel A. Kunin

I AM A board-certified urologic surgeon, in practice since 1966. In 1984, the Hebrew Union College-Jewish Institute of Religion in Los Angeles convened the first class of physicians and nurses trained to be non-Orthodox *mohalim/ot*—ritual circumcisers. I was part of that class and have been a practicing *mohel* in the southern California area ever since.

Brit milah—covenant of circumcision—is introduced in the Hebrew Bible in the book of Genesis, chapter 17. The only mandates listed are that circumcision is to be performed and that it must be done on the eighth day after the birth of a male child. There is no mention of how it should be performed, who must be present, or what prayers should be said.

Today's *brit milah* traditions are the result of a great deal of interpretation through the ages. There have been many changes, often paralleling dominant religious ideas brought on by external political, social, economic, and now scientific factors.

While the religious aspects of the ceremony have changed, the medical practice of circumcision has also evolved. It is difficult now to perceive how Abraham circumcised himself almost 4,000 years ago.

In an Orthodox community, life with its complex decisions can be relatively easy. If I were writing about *brit milah* for their community, a number of topics would be omitted. Defending the benefits of circumcision would be unnecessary because not circumcising would be out of the question. What types of clamps to be used and whether or not to administer anesthesia might be of interest but are essentially nonissues. No explanation would be needed as to why circumcision is done on the eighth day. It is expected. Discussion about egalitarian blessings, gay and lesbian families, patrilineal descent, and single-parent *britot* would not be welcomed.

However, I do not live or function in that world, and I suspect that most reading this book live as I do. I live in a more liberal, modern

---

1. Adapted from Samuel Kunin, *Circumcision: Its Place in Judaism, Past and Present* (Los Angeles: Isaac Nathan Publishing, 1998).

Jewish world—a highly complex world composed of many divisions. My Jewish world consists of Conservative, Reconstructionist, and Reform, which have within themselves wide variations, ranging from traditional to liberal. And then for good measure, it must also include all the non-affiliated members of the Jewish community.

These variations in Judaism have evolved because we are a people who constantly ask questions and often find different answers.

Some Religious Meanings of Brit Milah

The Hebrew words *brit* and *milah* mean "covenant" and "circumcision." *Webster's New Collegiate Dictionary* defines "covenant" as more than just a contract. It is a solemn and binding agreement, or a promise between two or more persons for the performance of some action. Circumcision is defined as the removal of the male foreskin or prepuce. *Brit milah* thus becomes the "covenant of circumcision."

The ceremony is primarily derived from the book of Genesis, chapter 17. God makes the following pact with Abraham: If Abraham circumcises Isaac on the eighth day and teaches Isaac to circumcise his son on the eighth day and this covenant is continued throughout the generations, God will ensure that Abraham's lineage will be fruitful, multiplying like the stars in the heavens, and Canaan will always be their homeland. The circumcision will forever be a sign of this covenant between God and Abraham.

For nearly 4,000 years this contract has been renewed by Jews even when doing so was punishable by death. It holds such significance that even Spinoza, the seventeenth-century Jewish philosopher [who raised significant doubts about the divine authority of the Torah], said, "The sign of circumcision is . . . so important . . . it alone would preserve the nation forever" (*Tractatus Theologico-Politicus* [1670] 3:53).

A certain philosopher once asked Rabbi Hoshaiah (second century c.e.): If God wants males circumcised, why did He not create them that way? Rabbi Hoshaiah answered: God creates wheat and man makes bread. Similarly, even man needs fixing through circumcision (Genesis Rabbah 11:6). Thus circumcision symbolizes that the Jewish mission is to fix the world.

When my sons became *b'nai mitzvah*, we were encouraged to write creative services. We were given the basic core of blessings that must be included and encouraged to augment them with any prayers, readings, or songs that we thought were significant.

And so it is with *brit milah*. Attend an Orthodox *brit,* and you will probably experience the basic core of prayers with little added, as it has been done for centuries. However, *brit milah* is thousands of years old, so we can be sure that it has been and is still evolving. Contemporary Jews have chosen to make what has been a mysterious and often frightening ceremony into a warm, understandable, educational, and even user-friendly experience.

The Prevalence of Circumcision

Circumcision is currently practiced by one sixth of the world's population. All of Islam circumcises males, but usually at a later age because Ishmael was circumcised at thirteen years. African tribes are known to circumcise as a rite of passage into manhood. In the well-known *Roots,* by Alex Haley, Kunta Kinta goes through such a ritual. Australian Aborigines, ancient Aztecs and Mayans, North and South American Indians, and some island people in both the Pacific and Indian Oceans did, or still circumcise. All Philippine Catholic boys are currently circumcised between eight to ten years of age.

We have found some clues to the origins of circumcision in the World War II North African experience and later with Operation Desert Storm (1991–1992). In both campaigns, balanitis—infection of the foreskin—was a significant problem. The combination of heat, sand, and infrequent bathing probably led to this condition. It was also a problem in the South Pacific during World War II; and as a result, the most frequent shipboard operation was circumcision.

As a U.S. Navy urologist assigned to the Marines at Camp Pendleton, California, during the Vietnam War, not a week passed that I was not asked to circumcise marines who were preparing to go to Vietnam. Stories of "jungle rot" of the penis were common, and these marines did not want to take any chances.

Medical Benefits of Circumcision

Edgar J. Schoen, M.D., was the chairman of the commission (of the American Academy of Pediatrics [AAP]) that studied the data and correctly concluded that there are benefits of circumcision in every decade of a man's life. His pediatric and neonatology experiences combined with my urologic background allow us to survey these benefits throughout a man's life.

1. Thomas Wiswell, M.D., a U.S. Army neonatologist, set out to prove there were no benefits from circumcision. However, in studying over

200,000 male infants, he found, to his surprise, that newborn males had more severe urinary tract infections than girls and that these infections were ten to twenty times more common in uncircumcised boys. Urinary tract infections, particularly in the neonatal period, often result in kidney damage and scarring. Since his study, Dr. Wiswell has become a strong proponent of circumcision, and subsequently his findings have been independently corroborated.

2. As boys develop, up to 12 percent of them will have some type of problem with their foreskins that will require either medical or surgical treatment. Some are local irritations or infections. Others are mechanical problems, including

   a. *Phimosis,* the inability of the foreskin to retract naturally by puberty. When this is particularly tight, the foreskin may balloon during urination due to partial obstruction. Treatment requires surgery, almost always performed under a general anesthesia in this age group.

   b. *Paraphimosis,* which occurs when the foreskin is pulled down the shaft of the penis and cannot be returned to its normal position. When this occurs, swelling of the tight foreskin occurs and literally strangles the shaft of the penis. If it cannot be manually reduced, immediate surgical repair is indicated.

   c. Infections under a foreskin, which may result in permanent adhesions of the inside of the foreskin to the head of the penis. If left alone, this may impair sexual function at a later date and create disfiguring scars.

3. As a boy advances into his sexually active years, there is always the danger of sexually transmitted diseases (STDs). The moist, enclosed undersurface of the foreskin is a perfect breeding ground for these diseases. If the young man cannot, or will not, inspect and clean himself, he may not even realize he has a problem until it is far advanced. By far, the worst cases of STDs I have seen are in uncircumcised men. Although all forms of STDs are alarming, two require particular attention:

   a. During the 1980s, reports from Kenya showed that uncircumcised men exposed to HIV-positive prostitutes had anywhere from three to eight times greater chances of becoming HIV positive than circumcised men. It is not unusual to contract more than one

STD, and further reports found that the risk was increased if they already had a sore on their foreskin from diseases like syphilis and chancroid. These figures have been substantiated several times in other studies—for example, similar findings have been found among homosexual men in Seattle. Due to these results, circumcision has been suggested for boys and men in Africa in order to control the AIDS epidemic. Thousands of African men have been and are being circumcised, and programs have been initiated for infant circumcision.

b. When I was a boy growing up in the 1950s, I was told that women who were married to Jewish men did not get cancer of the cervix. This was refuted in the 1971 AAP policy statement on circumcision. They suggested that increased sexual promiscuity with multiple sexual partners was a more likely cause. However, over the years, a connection with certain strains of the human papilloma virus (HPV), more commonly known as venereal warts, has been identified and linked with cancer of the cervix. When women are infected with HPV, a chronic irritation and thinning of the cervix occurs, which is a precursor to cancer. Worse, HPV is often very small and not easily seen, particularly inside the foreskin, so a man may not even know he has it. Therefore, an all-too-common condition may result in disaster for an unknowing sexual partner many years after the fact. The Center for Communicable Diseases predicts that up to 30 percent of teenagers will contract some form of STD.

4. Cancer of the penis is a rare condition, occurring in 1 in 50,000 males in America. No man circumcised at birth has ever had cancer of the penis. In certain areas of South America, up to 25 percent of male cancers were penile in origin. These are in native areas, where local hygiene is poor. Penile cancer occurs as early as in the third decade of life and is a very aggressive, painful, and often fatal disease.

5. As men grow older, sexual difficulty and irritation may occur due to progressive scarring from chronic infections. One of the common causes of such infections is diabetes, which makes a man more prone to infections in general and specifically under the foreskin. I have often been called to nursing homes to reduce a paraphomosis caused by an agitated patient pulling on his foreskin. This requires immediate

63

surgical reduction. An even more common problem in this patient group is the inability of nurses to pass catheters because of tight foreskins. External condom catheters on these patients are a disaster because of almost guaranteed infections.

I certainly agree with Dr. Schoen's suggestion that circumcision has protective powers in every decade of a male's life. The data are overwhelming and have not been disproved by any claims of anti-circumcision advocates.

On the contrary, Dr. Brian Morris of the School of Medical Sciences at the University of Sydney has recently (July 2007) summarized the current medical data (available at www.circinfo.net), indicating that circumcision has benefits for both men and their female sexual partners:

Benefits to Women of Male Circumcision

The load of infectious bacteria and viruses that accumulate under the foreskin is delivered into the female genital tract during sex. This means that if the male partner is circumcised, there is

- A fivefold reduction in the risk of cervical cancer (which is caused by the human papilloma virus)

- A fivefold reduction in risk of a woman being infected by *Chlamydia trachomatis*. Chlamydia has more than doubled over the past five years and can cause infertility (in both sexes), pelvic inflammatory disease, and ectopic pregnancy.

- A twofold reduction in risk of Herpes simplex type 2 (genital herpes).

- A reduced risk of other sexually transmitted infections such as HIV/AIDS, syphilis, and chancroid because it is less likely that the male has any of these.

- Better hygiene, including no malodorous smegma.

- No phimosis, which refers to a tight foreskin that cannot be pulled back fully. This occurs in 1 in 10 uncircumcised men and makes erections, and thus sexual intercourse, difficult or impossible. Because these men also find cleaning under the foreskin difficult, hygiene is poor.

- Improved sexual pleasure. There are various reasons for this. Research shows women prefer the appearance of a circumcised penis as well as the fact that it is cleaner and is, therefore, preferred for oral sex.

During intercourse, there is increased penile and vaginal contact and stimulation, and the circumcised man may "last" slightly longer. Research also indicates a greater likelihood of the woman reaching an orgasm if the man is circumcised.

Benefits to Men and Boys of Circumcision

- Eliminates the risk of phimosis, a condition in which cleaning under the foreskin, and passing urine, is difficult and painful. Phimosis also greatly increases the risk of penile cancer and is the cause of foreskin and catheter problems in nursing homes.

- Reduces by threefold the risk of inflammation and infection of the skin of the penis. One in ten uncircumcised men suffer from inflammation of the head of the penis and foreskin some time in their lives. This rises to one in three if the uncircumcised man is diabetic. (Diabetic men also have other severe problems when uncircumcised.) In contrast, only 2 percent of circumcised men experience such inflammation.

- Substantially reduces the risk of urinary tract infections (UTIs). In infancy the risk of UTI is only 1 in 500 if the boy is circumcised. In contrast, 1 in 50 uncircumcised male infants will get a UTI. This very painful condition is particularly dangerous in infancy and in 40 percent of cases can lead to kidney inflammation and disease; sepsis and meningitis can also result. UTI is the cause of fever in 25 percent of febrile male infants who are uncircumcised but in only 1 percent of circumcised boys.

- Over twenty-fold decrease in risk of invasive penile cancer, which has a high fatality rate. Of uncircumcised men, 1 in 600 get penile cancer, which often requires penile amputation or disfiguring surgery, leading to impaired penile function.

- Significant studies suggest that uncircumcised men have one and a half to two times the risk of prostate cancer, which affects one in six men.

- Reduces by approximately threefold to sevenfold the risk of getting HIV/AIDS during sex with an infected woman. HIV enters via the vulnerable inner lining of the foreskin of a healthy penis but can also infect via sores anywhere on the penis (caused, for example, by genital herpes, balanitis, or inflammation). The man's risk, especially if uncircumcised, will be greater if he engages in unsafe sex with individuals at high risk for HIV infection. Condoms should always be used irrespective of circumcision status.

- Provides substantial protection against thrush, as well as sexually transmitted infections such as papilloma (wart) virus, syphilis, and chancroid.

- Up to 10 percent of males reaching adulthood uncircumcised will later require circumcision for medical reasons. Many are reluctant to go ahead with this or are incorrectly advised to "put up" with the problem rather than have a circumcision. Early elective circumcision eliminates risk of these problems before they occur.

- Credible research shows that most women prefer the appearance of the circumcised penis. They also prefer it for sexual activity. Hygiene is one reason.

- There is no significant difference in sensitivity or sensation during an erection between a circumcised and uncircumcised penis.

- Failure to circumcise in infancy means stitches being used for circumcision of older children, teenagers, and adults. Delay past four months means progressive escalation in total cost.

In sum, our ancestors had important, religious reasons to circumcise their male infants, binding him to the covenant between God and Abraham long ago and continuing through the generations to our time. *Brit milah* thus connects us not only to God but to our people in the past, present, and future. We, in turn, are discovering new meanings in the ritual, ones that reflect our own era and family, thereby adding to its value for us. In addition, we now know that circumcision has major medical benefits for both men and women. For religious, ethnic, familial, and medical reasons, then, the ancient Jewish rite of *brit milah* is one well worth preserving.

Judaism, Body Image, and Food
Lori Hope Lefkovitz

R OOTED IN the Garden of Eden is the idea that we are beings who must, but cannot, resist temptation. Contemporary manifestations of this message are everywhere, reiterated by the diet industry, advertisers, poets, and painters. Woman's hunger and insatiability; her lack of self-control and disobedience; her power to reason men out of their better judgment; and her vulnerability to misleading, beguiling serpent-types emit the ancient ring of "truth." The problems of food and sex would seem to have begun at the beginning.

Like most time-honored systems of meaning, Judaism has participated in the making of our culture, and it has been one source for negative cultural values, attitudes, and stereotypes. But Judaism is also a counter-tradition with potential to provide antidotes to popular culture and be a resource for health. With a twist of the interpretive lens, the Garden of Eden can be understood to exemplify healthy adolescence: growing up and leaving the abundance of childhood to make one's way in the world; needing to break the protective rules of childhood and responsibly face a life of adult trials by working and nurturing life; staying close to your partner, your parents, and your God; always being prepared to forgive and be forgiven.

Besides being home to the snake, that same garden was home to the first rose—which would eventually signify romantic love—and the first chicken from which, eventually, the shtetl *bubbes* would make their chicken soup. Saturated with cultural connotations, even a chicken is not just a chicken. For that chicken soup is a symbol of therapeutic Judaism: maternal love; the kitchen's warmth; a broth with infinite potential to cure whatever ails your body, spirit, or psyche. I am convinced that everything—including our bodies and our desires—has a history and is a product of that history. So, basic as food and sex might seem, they have become culturally complicated.

This essay is about the way the body and the desires of the Jewish woman entered our collective imagination as a biblical inheritance. It is also about Jewish traditions and practices that can serve as an antidote to our culture's destructive attitudes toward food and body. The Jewish diet on which many of us were raised has some bitter ingredients to swallow in a tradition of heroines whose example may have led us to internalize negative stereotypes of the Jewish woman that may have led to feelings of shame and self-disgust. But other aspects of this ethnic diet—Jewish traditions and practices—promote healthy attitudes toward food and balanced living that support our well being and self worth.

In the Hebrew Bible, whenever a hero has a story about his birth, the story begins with a barren mother. This is an unlikely story, of course: mothers, by definition, are not barren. Except for Leah, the matriarchs, the first Jewish mothers, are all barren, infertile, empty. Samson's mother and the mother of the great prophet Samuel are barren too. Their stories begin with desperation and longing, a life-hunger that cannot be satisfied by themselves or the people who love them.

Typically, these empty mothers enter into an implicit pact with the Divine. Because of the mother's special arrangement with God, her son is preferred over his older, stronger brothers. Sarah—the first matriarch and a mother in old age—protects her child, Isaac, by insisting, over her husband Abraham's objections, on expelling Abraham's firstborn, Ishmael, from their home. Rebekah tricks her husband into preferring Jacob over the outdoorsman and hunter Esau, and Rachel waits long bitter years for the birth of the younger, favored Joseph.

From longing to loss. These women, whose principle role is as wives and mothers, protect and promote their weaker sons only to give them up to God's larger plans. Sarah dies immediately after Isaac is brought for a near sacrifice; Jacob must flee home for fear of his brother Esau's revenge; Joseph is sold by his brothers into slavery, and then Rachel dies in childbirth with her next and last child; Samuel is given over to temple service after he is weaned. The mother longs for a son, becomes his principle protector, and then watches as he leaves her to take *his* place in history.

In this type of the matriarch, we find the origins of the 20th Jewish mother stereotype. "It's okay, she'll sit in the dark." These Mrs. Portnoys are ambitious for their boys and controlling in ways that compromise the power and potency of their husbands and sons. And when their boys do achieve independence, they feel a neglect that resonates with the losses of Jewish mothers over the ages. She induces quiet, disabling guilt: "I don't want anything for myself, but after all I have done for you . . . "

The Hebrew Bible offers us another prototype of womanhood, a type of character who appears any number of times. This one is not a mother, but instead acts in the political arena. She appears as Delilah, as Yael, as

Judith, and as Queen Esther—and her role is always to achieve a military victory in the bedroom. She lures the man into her tent, and even if he is the strongest man on earth, her seductions are effective enough to undo him. In Samson's case, though he defeats armies and lions with his bare hands, Delilah's beauty and whining reduce him to a blinded, shorn Oedipus, symbolically castrated by his own weakness for perfume.

Yael lures the enemy General Sisera into her tent, gives him milk when he asks for water, and then surprises the reader and Sisera alike by penetrating him when we expect her to be penetrated. She drives a tent pin through his temple, as the story tells us, "until it reaches the ground" and thus achieves victory for the Hebrews.

Queen Esther marries a king who does not know she is a Jew; and when her people come under a death sentence, she agrees to conceal her sadness, doll herself up, and—at risk to her own life—seek an audience with the king. Three times she appears uninvited before the king, "touches his royal scepter," and finds favor in his sight. Through these manipulations and some successful parties, she saves her people from destruction.

Judith is a beautiful widow. When the city is under siege and surrounded, she dresses herself in her fanciest attire and slips out the city gates. She locates the enemy General Holofernes and offers herself to him, presumably to save herself. When he has drunk himself into an enthusiastic stupor, she cuts off his head, carries it home in a bag, and sets up a dramatic display on the hilltop. With the morning light, the enemy sees its leader's head on a stick and flees. The Hebrews are saved.

What I want to emphasize is that this character is imagined to exercise sexual power over men, but she does not feel the desire to which she pretends. In fact, she is alienated from her desires because her goals are not personal. Esther, Yael, and Judith dress up to allure others; they offer handsome promises, but their effect is destructive.

We recognize her twentieth-century descendant in the insincere, overly well-dressed Jewish American Princess. This terrifying (and frightened), manicured girl from Long Island can get whatever she wants from her daddy, and men on campus know well that she is to be avoided because she can eat you up alive. While she may seem to have little in common with the self-sacrificing Jewish mother, both types compromise the masculinity of the men in their lives. Although the princess is forever dieting (just as Queen Esther spent months undergoing beauty treatments) and the Jewish mother is forever demanding that we eat, both are manipulative because they are themselves empty with unmet longings. Forever hungry, the princess grows up finally to become her mother: the Jewish mother who promotes her sons in the interest of vicariously enjoying his power.

These types are real, of course, only in our cultural imagination. They haunt us as shadow selves, and they tell us about our own unconscious attitudes and internalized anti-Semitism: Jewish men are imagined to be weak relative to the bigger, older, more brawny Ishmaels and Esaus of the dominant culture. The stereotypes partly express and transfer this anxiety onto the competing characterizations of Jewish women.

There is nothing inevitable about these characterizations. But Jewish women may well feel themselves living in reaction to the attitudes and images that have become part of the collective unconscious. The Jewish woman is not necessarily relaxed about how she is perceived. She fulfills these negative prophecies, or she lives in rebellion against them. Her esteem is compromised. She may feel unloved in spite of evidence to the contrary. She may swallow her sadness, or she may shrink herself because she feels like the biggest, loudest person in the room even if she has not said a word.

I do not mean to suggest that there is truth in these generalizations, and I do not mean to suggest that similarly split images of women—virgins and whores—are not prevalent in other places in Western culture. Low self-esteem and eating disorders are prevalent in girls and women generally in our society, but these images are the particular origins and expressions of Jewish women's self-dissatisfaction and sometimes self-loathing.

When we internalize the negative messages of our culture, they have power over us and attack us from within. If we feel ourselves to be vaguely, anxiously "too Jewish," or if we work hard so as not to appear to be "too Jewish" in a society that does not appreciate Jewishness, then we are at the mercy of anti-Semitic stereotypes.

My teacher Allen Grossman used to say that we read the great books of our civilization not to ingest them but rather to get them out of our system. We unconsciously consume the myths of our culture. By reading and studying, we put ourselves in a position to be critical; to reinterpret that which is problematic; and to reclaim what we discover that is worthy, useful, and even redemptive.

So too with our Jewish inheritance. We may be aware that Jewish law and legend, as we have received it, often devalues women and the female body. But if we engage in acts of critical reading and revision, we can extend beyond disowning the legacy that fears barren mothers or female bleeding. Instead, we discover the tradition's greater system of values. In Jewish ritual, holidays, symbols, ideas, and beliefs are much of what we need to develop a loving and wholesome relationship to ourselves.

The practices that I discuss in the following paragraphs are meant to suggest merely some of the possibilities for blessing, for holiness and wholeness within a long and richly textured tradition. Traditional Jewish practice encourages mindfulness, attention to the details of the gifts of our bodies, our well-being, and the earth. The morning blessings that are meant to be recited daily include a litany of small things for which we are grateful, including, remarkably, the openings and closings in our bodies. We should not take these holes for granted, the prayers remind us, because it is terrible trouble when any one of them is not working well.

The foods of Jewish holidays provide nourishment for body, mind, and spirit. At Rosh Hashanah, we savor apples and honey that we may ingest the hope for life's sweetest of blessings. We eat round challot, reminding us of the cycles of birth and life in the season of therapeutic self-reflection that commemorates the birthday of the world.

The weekly Sabbath table includes two braided breads. We eat from two breads to remind us of the double portion of manna—nourishment—miraculously available to the Hebrews wandering through the desert in the Exodus myth. This symbol of manna in the breads is an invitation to us to be grateful for life's bounty, a reminder of the time in our own infancy when nourishment was provided for us in an unencumbered, uncomplicated way. We cried and were fed. Judaism legislates that on the Sabbath, one must eat three complete meals, a sign of the day's holiness.

At Yom Kippur, and a few select other solemn days, we fast. This fasting, by contrast with the cultural restricting of food intake called dieting, is a spiritual practice. You may not fast to lose weight or to punish yourself. You may not fast if you are ill, pregnant, nursing, or recovering. Because the fast is rule governed and strictly limited, it is a marked corrective to the counterproductive and often self-destructive practices of diets or more exaggerated fasts.

On Sukkot we celebrate first fruits and the season of planting. We build booths in memory of living in the fields and to demonstrate that we can carry our homes along with us. We show that home and comfort with ourselves is located wherever we happen to be. By remembering that our ancestors built temporary shelters in the fields, we recall the centrality of nourishing the body; and today, we often use the occasion of gratitude for the shelter that we enjoy to attend to those who are homeless.

We celebrate four new years. One is Tu B'shvat, the new year of trees. Again, special foods, the fruits and nuts of the land of Israel, are eaten to honor the trees and to invite our gratitude for the peculiar bounty of our land.

The two, principle *mitzvot*—commandments—associated with Esther's holiday, Purim, concern food. A feast must be prepared and eaten, and gift baskets containing at least three different kinds of food should be given to friends. Community is thereby defined in the practice of sharing food, a metaphor for the importance of reciprocity and the centrality of gift exchange in Jewish community.

The holiday cycle is a kind of food pyramid that emphasizes balance. From the apples and honey of Rosh Hashanah and the fruits and grains of Sukkot, Hanukkah is the holiday of oils and fats. Reminding us of the miracle of the oil that lasted eight days, we are invited to eat the miraculous in the form of foods fried in oil: latkes for some of us and, in Israel, jelly donuts. On the harvest festival of Shavuot, it is customary to refrain from eating meat and to enjoy dairy foods, with an emphasis on blintzes in some communities. On this holiday we read the pastoral story of the book of Ruth, a story that begins with famine, loss, and depletion and that concludes in the wheat fields with abundance, fertility, and the promise of ultimate fulfillment and redemption.

Passover, the spring festival, is rich in food symbolism. The Seder (the Hebrew word for "order") expresses liberation through ordered eating. "All who are hungry" are invited to eat. The bread is a "bread of affliction" to remind us of the various kinds of enslavement that we suffer. Saltwater stands for bitter tears, cups brimming with wine symbolize the contrasting bounty of the redemption that we are commanded to celebrate; a sweet mixture of fruit, wine, and walnuts represents mortar; and we literally swallow the herbs that will make us taste bitterness. Significantly, the work of the Seder, like the work of many Jewish religious occasions, is to retell our own stories, to repeat them over and again. We are asked to eat thoughtfully and to be present in our collective pasts. Repeating one's personal story, family story, and communal story is the therapeutic practice of developing a positive self identity.

Jewish eating, classically, begins always with a blessing over the food, a simple formula that acknowledges a life source from which come the grain from the ground and fruits from the vine, the trees, or the earth. Like the grace after meals and the regulations of kashrut—the laws of keeping kosher—these practices encourage a grateful attitude and eating habits that are at once disciplined and joyful. In Jewish religious, ritual, and liturgical practice, food is a blessing and eating is sanctified. In the Jewish textual tradition, the body is a tabernacle and sanctuary. Alternatively, the body is the image of God.

Today, many Jewish women in particular are reviving or reinventing practices that honor the female body in a Jewish idiom. Just as the Bible describes a weaning party for Isaac, contemporary weaning ceremonies for nursing mothers and babies often take place at *Havdalah,* the ceremony that separates the Sabbath from the days of the week. In this ritual of separation, the baby may be given his or her first *Kiddush Cup* to symbolize the need to seek nourishment independent of the mother's body. The cup is given with the wish that it brim over with life's blessings.

At puberty, when girls often feel diminished personal power, the bat mitzvah ceremony celebrates in community a public display of Jewish learning, chanting, and speaking, a significant corrective to those social messages that tell young girls to look pretty and avoid showing off.

Rosh Hodesh groups, reviving an ancient women's festival associated with the lunar cycles of a woman's fertile body, celebrate the strength that women can acquire in community. Whether it is a revival of the cleansing rituals of the fresh-water bath of the *mikveh* or the invention of croning ceremonies that remind us of the matriarch Sarah's wisdom and power in her latter years, and offer that example for contemporary women to follow, a new class of books by women mark our life-cycle moments Jewishly, by using the Jewish textual tradition in order to promote personal and collective strength and health, affirm life, and honor what is best in the traditions of our ancestors.

Reclaiming the Body: Anorexia and Bulimia in the Jewish Community

Judith Rabinor

"To save one life is to save the world."
    —The Mishnah (Sanhedrin 4:5)

"MY FILTHY habit kicked in again!" A tearful Naomi sank into the couch in my office. "I must be crazy!" It was the day after the second Seder, and she had been free from binging and purging for several months. "The first Seder was a total pig-out, so I decided I'd stick to salad and vegetables last night," she said. But when she saw the pot roast and roast potatoes, the chicken and kugel, she lost control. Although she ate only a mouthful of each, within moments, she excused herself from the table, slipped into the bathroom where she proceeded to throw everything up. "I couldn't help it," she said ruefully, "I felt so fat."

Naomi, a thirty-one-year-old Jewish mother of six-year-old twin girls, has struggled with food, weight, and her body since early childhood when she was labeled "chubby." As an overweight teen, she began dieting; by college, the relentless pursuit of thinness had spun into a full blown anorexia nervosa. In response to feeling starved, she began binging. Next came vomiting. Before long she was bulimic.

Naomi is not alone in her unhealthy relationship with food, eating, and the body. From being overweight to being anorexic and then bulimic, Naomi has spent most of her life battling with food and body. Although most women do not have life-threatening eating disorders, the majority of females spend a lifetime feeling guilty about what they eat and agonizing over their bodies.

We are born hungry; and forever, until we take our last breath, we must learn to nourish our hungers, appetites, and desires, our mind, body, and soul. How has what began as a sacred right—feeding ourselves—become, for so many women, a dreaded taboo?

I am a clinical psychologist who has spent over thirty years working with people—mostly women—who have struggled with eating and body image disorders. These complex conditions arise from a combination of behavioral, biological, genetic, emotional; and sociocultural factors. While they are exacerbated by our culture's obsession with weight loss, an eating disorder is always about more than an obsession with dieting and one's body. Starving, chronic dieting, binging, excessive exercising, and being preoccupied with fat thoughts are the tip of an emotional iceberg. My work is always about helping people identify and nourish the unmet emotional, psychological, and spiritual hungers masked and expressed in these behaviors.

As many as 10 million females and 1 million males fight a daily battle with anorexia and bulimia, a life-threatening eating disorder whose complications claim the lives of 5 to 10 percent of sufferers each year. At any given time, 10 percent or more of adolescent girls and adult women report disordered eating—behaviors characterized by excessive dieting and exercising that, although not diagnosable eating disorders, cause seriously impaired lifestyles. Once thought to effect predominately teenage girls, anorexia and bulimia occur throughout the life cycle and affect males as well as females. In addition to anorexia and bulimia, more than 25 million people struggle with binge-eating disorder, often a precursor to obesity.

In the psychotherapy session that followed, Naomi and I explored her binge–purge. The middle of five children, Naomi grew up feeling invisible, sandwiched between an older sister, known as "The Brain," and a younger sister who was the prettiest and most popular girl in her class.

"My mom's Seder table brought up my old feelings of envy, competition, and inadequacy," she realized. Feeling shamed, silenced, and invisible, she turned to her tools of survival: binging and purging. Unable to control unacceptable thoughts and feelings, Naomi used food to sooth herself. Later, she distracted herself by throwing up. For Naomi, binging and purging were her tools of emotional survival. Learning to identify, accept, and talk about her shameful feelings, rather than stuff them down her mouth or deposit them in the toilet was the beginning of her healing journey.

No one theory explains the development of eating and body image disorders. Although the cultural emphasis on thinness undeniably damages all women, only a small percentage develops diagnosable eating problems. These disorders serve different functions for different people at different stages. They generally help one avoid dealing with unacceptable feelings, moods, and thoughts by keeping obsessive fat thoughts and food-related behaviors in the forefront of one's consciousness. They can be triggered by peer and family issues as well as by a host of traumatic events, including emotional, physical, and sexual abuse. While they occur throughout the life cycle, onset is most often in adolescence, when teens and young adults are faced with a host of new physiological changes, cognitive demands, and social and emotional pressures. Ultimately, these disorders have more to do with coping with one's thoughts and feelings than with one's body.

Jewish Vulnerabilities and Genetic Disposition

As a psychotherapist, I try to help each person unlock the mysterious needs hidden behind his or her eating problem. Learning how to truly nourish oneself is the goal of therapy. While women from all countries and cultures develop eating disorders, Jewish women face unique challenges and vulnerabilities. Like all Americans, Jews are exposed to pervasive media images pressuring women to achieve an unachievable standard of thinness. On a daily basis, we are bombarded with unrealistic images of the female body in newspapers, television, and magazines. These images promote eating and body image disorders. Feeling fat is the norm for the majority of American women when compared to images of ultra-thin models who are tall, blond, lean, and lanky. For most females, and especially Jewish women whose genes predispose them to being short, stocky, and dark, making peace with one's body is especially challenging.

The Role of Food and Mealtime in Jewish Life

"My binges began with the Hanukkah latkas."

"It was the Yom Kippur fast that led to my anorexia."

The central role food plays in Jewish life creates a compounded vulnerability for Jewish women. From fasting on Yom Kippur to overeating on Shabbat and Passover, a cornerstone of Jewish identity has always been rituals that involve family meals. For Jews, food has always had multiple meanings of survival and resilience. Not only do unique Jewish dishes celebrate the cycles of life but mealtime itself tells the story of Jews as a persecuted, migratory people. Often forced by pogroms to leave their homes on a moment's notice, only what could be carried on one's back was taken. Often a pair of candlesticks and a tablecloth were all that remained of their vanished lives and became the centerpiece of a new home and life. Mealtime was symbolic of resiliency in the face of persecution. Even today, for many Jews, saying a blessing over bread and wine evokes memories of loss and hope and simultaneously celebrates the continuity of life itself.

76

The Orthodox Community

Women in the certain sects of the Orthodox community face special risks. Strictly prescribed roles often define their lives. They are under great pressure to marry early; and arranged marriages, immediate child-bearing, and large families are the norm. For example, Orna was a young woman who was pushed to start husband hunting at 17; feeling unready for marriage, the search triggered a deadly diet. For young girls who are unprepared to start families, anorexia is a way to delay puberty, put off childbearing, and gain control of their bodies when their lives are out of their control.

Because many psychological problems such as addictions, alcoholism, and eating disorders carry a stigma, often anorexics and their families keep their problems secret and avoid identifying the problem or seeking psychotherapy until the problems are dangerously severe. One particularly upsetting experience with an Orthodox family stands out. Rifka, a twenty-four-year-old married woman with five small children, arrived at my office in a state of severe emaciation. She had come in at the urging of her mother, who suspected bulimia. Upon consultation, Rifka admitted to being bulimic and dated the onset of her bulimia to an unhappy marriage. She wanted to divorce her husband, but feared her parents would carry out their threat to disown her if she divorced. Although I attempted to educate her parents about the serious medical and emotional problems associated with her eating disorder, her mother stood firm: Divorce was taboo. "There are some things worse than bulimia," her mother stated flatly as she left my office, "and divorce is one."

Issues of Identity: Dieting as a Ritual of Female Identity

People develop a personal identity (e.g., familial, ethnic, religious, and occupational) based on both a need for uniqueness and for group affiliation. Many Jews struggle with the tension between assimilating with mainstream American culture and retaining a sense of Jewish identity. This tension can be played out with food and/or with dieting. For example, dieting can have multiple ways of strengthening one's personal identity. Consider eighteen-year-old Rebecca, who developed anorexia. It took many months of therapy before we were able to uncover the roots, hidden in her past. Eventually, Rebecca became aware that the origins of her feelings of "being unworthy to live" came from an unconscious identification with her maternal grandmother, lost in the Holocaust.

Throughout time and across cultures, rituals help negotiate life's transitions and strengthen one's sense of identity. Unfortunately, in contrast to rituals celebrating the male life cycle (circumcision, bar mitzvah), few rituals in Judaism celebrate the seasons of a woman's life. In mainstream culture, especially at adolescence, dieting is one of the few rituals that bond women, but it does so in a destructive way; it has even become a ritual of female identity, such that wherever women gather, there is inevitably talk about weight loss. For Jewish women, excessive dieting may reflect a need to rebel against one's Jewish heritage and genetic endowment as well as separate from a family that centers itself on food and eating.

Rituals of Renewal: How Jewish Practices Can Heal

I am probably more of a practicing therapist than a practicing Jew, yet I am steeped in many Jewish traditions that have enriched my life; and what enters my life, enters my work. Both Judaism and psychotherapy embrace the concepts of courage, compassion, and empathy as fundamental building blocks of growth. I bring many Jewish concepts into my work as a way of bonding with clients.

The Metaphor of the *Mishkan*. People with eating disorders are disconnected from themselves, others, and the universe. They need a safe place to reconnect and heal. When I begin therapy, I overtly invite each person into a *mishkan,* a "sacred dwelling place," where we can work together to reclaim the parts of himself or herself lost to the relentless pursuit of thinness. In addition, people with eating disorders benefit from being reminded that their bodies are sacred. Healing involves reclaiming one's body as a *mishkan,* a sacred dwelling place.

The *Mi Shebairach*. Debbie Friedman's contemporary rendition of the *Mi Shebairach,* a prayer of healing, reminds us to "Help us find the courage to make our lives a blessing." Many people who suffer from eating disorders benefit from using these healing words as daily affirmations. "I eat to fill the hole in my soul," were the words of Maya, a thirty-two-year-old woman who introduced herself to me as spiritually bankrupt. Integrating meaningful spiritual concepts to sufferers can be a source of great spiritual nourishment.

Rosh Hodesh. In the past few decades, a growing number of Jewish women have focused on developing rituals honoring the feminine. One example is the revival of the ancient ceremony celebrating the new moon,

Rosh Hodesh. From Talmudic times, Jewish tradition designated Rosh Hodesh as a special holiday, when women gathered to feast, celebrate, and pray. Today Rosh Hodesh groups create new rituals as well as recover neglected ones. Some groups celebrate biblical women such as Judith and Miriam; others invent new rituals to celebrate unique aspects of women's lives, such as pregnancy, labor, and childbirth as well as to grieve losses, such as miscarriages. New groups are tailored for girls and teens, hoping to foster Jewish identity and boost self-esteem at a time when stick-thin models make many young girls feel bad about their bodies.

Holy Sparks. The Kabbalah teaches us to search for our shattered sparks, the parts of us we have lost. This concept is particularly useful for my work with people struggling with eating disorders. For example, Rena, a former patient, had been bulimic at age twenty-one. She recalled a despairing moment of her life. In a session she had asked me, "Will I ever get better? Do you think I can recover?" She was touched deeply by a quote that I found attributed to Rabbi Nachman of Breslov: "As long as a tiny flame remains, a great fire can be rekindled." I reminded her of, and gently drew her attention to, many of her inner resources. The mystics believed that we will attain wholeness by finding our holy sparks. This concept is akin to a strength-based approach that guides my work as a psychotherapist.

Storytelling. One of my tools as a psychotherapist is also at the heart of Judaism. I encourage my patients to think about and tell the stories of their lives. Jews have a deep respect for storytelling. Each year Jews read the Torah from cover to cover, always certain that each rereading will offer new meanings. Passover, the holiday most celebrated by Jews worldwide, is based on the retelling of the story of freedom. Like Judaism, psychotherapy is based on the principle that each time a person tells his or her story, new meanings are revealed. Certainly this has great relevance to eating disorders, for binging and starving always contain a hidden story.

Forgiveness. One of the final steps of recovery often involves asking for forgiveness from oneself. I often initiate the practice of *Selichot* (petitions for forgiveness) into my work. Although this practice of asking for forgiveness from those we have harmed usually occurs between Rosh Hashanah and Yom Kippur, it may be practiced anytime. This practice teaches that if one asks three times for forgiveness from someone

one has harmed, forgiveness must be granted. It reminds us not to hold grudges, that anger destroys. People with eating disorders tend to be perfectionists and often have great difficulty forgiving themselves. The ritual of *Selichot* can be used to encourage self-forgiveness.

Conclusion

The world breaks everyone and afterwards, some of us are strong in the broken places.

—Ernest Hemingway

The idealization of thinness damages all of us. It is about being who you are supposed to be instead of being who you are. Judaism and psychotherapy teach people to celebrate life, value the present moment, and honor what is holy/whole. Healing involves helping patients know that who they are is enough. I remind my patients of an old Hassidic tale. Before his death, Rabbi Zusya said, "In the coming world, they will not ask me 'Why were you not Moses?' They will ask me, 'Why were you not Zusya?'" The aim of psychotherapy is to try to help our patients become strong in the broken places. The unexpected gift of being a therapist is that when my patients grow, I grow. This is the essence of *tikkun olum:* We are all always repairing a communal brokenness.

Physicians' Perspectives

Desta's Heart: A Difficult Case of Caring

Judith Levitan

D ESTA IS a 38-year-old new patient for me, asking for help getting pregnant. Both her liveliness and her rapid-fire, accented, lilting speech fills more space than her four-foot, eleven-inch, 107-pound frame would suggest. I instantly like her. Born and raised in Ethiopia, she developed rheumatic heart disease as a child. If she had been lucky enough to be diagnosed and corrected at a young age, she would have done very well. When she was sixteen, the charitable arm of the local university brought her to the United States for corrective heart surgery, a mechanical mitral heart valve replacement. Nevertheless, significant damage to her heart had already occurred, and she was deemed too ill to ever live in Ethiopia, although she had been back many times to visit.

At age 32 she became pregnant and underwent an elective abortion at the advice of her obstetrician and cardiologist. She now regrets that decision and feels she was coerced into it. At age 37 she became pregnant again and spontaneously miscarried. Since the dilation and curettage (D&C) for the miscarriage, her menses have been nonexistent or are just light spotting. The workup and testing I do show Asherman's syndrome: the front and back walls of the uterus have scarred together, eliminating the endometrium (the uterine lining). The timing strongly suggests that Asherman's was a complication of the D&C.

Desta's marriage is troubled. Her old records were transferred to me, so I know that her husband has asked for a divorce in the past. She is tearful when she tells me she considered suicide after her recent D&C because she feared being unable to give her husband a child. Her desire to deliver a child is so overwhelming that she is willing to expose herself to a significant risk of dying in the process.

Desta's risk of death in pregnancy is somewhere between 10 and 50 percent because her heart disease is now severe. She has an intractable arrhythmia with a history of two ventricular fibrillation cardiac arrests. One of the medications she used for her arrhythmia, amiodarone, has had some negative effects on her lungs, giving her a mild form of emphysema. She has congestive heart failure, meaning her heart is dilated and does not pump efficiently. In pregnancy, the mother's heart and lungs must work harder than usual, but Desta's cardiopulmonary capacity barely sustains her now. Hence her baby will likely be born very early, with all the attendant risks of prematurity.

I dig deeper, trying to discern why she is willing to risk her health and her potential child's life. Our discussion is long. She is emphatic that she does not fear physical harm from her husband or divorce if she cannot have children. They cannot afford a gestational carrier; in this special form of in vitro fertilization an embryo is created from her eggs and her husband's sperm and then implanted in another woman's uterus. Desta is not interested in adoption.

Her identity and self-worth are very contingent upon her ability to successfully bear children. This is not strictly an Ethiopian cultural value. She was very lonely during her first years in the United States. With the recent influx of immigrants from Ethiopia, she finally has a community, but she still feels like an outsider. She believes having a child will help her standing in the community.

In Desta, the surgical treatment for Asherman's would be dangerous. In that surgery, the uterus is dilated with fluid under pressure, the cervix is cannulated with a scope, and the adhesions between the front and back walls of the uterus are cut with electrocautery. Because cautery uses electricity, a thick sugar solution is used to distend the uterus so the current will not carry elsewhere. In widely varying amounts, this fluid is adsorbed and can cause tremendous fluid shifts in the body that challenge a healthy person. Such a phenomenon could certainly kill Desta. Modern monitoring techniques would help but are imperfect.

Her artificial heart valve creates other risks that seem minor in comparison. She has to be on anticoagulants, blood thinners, to avoid developing a clot that could break off and cause a stroke. This is temporarily reversed for surgery. During pregnancy, the medication is changed from a pill to an injectable drug to avoid birth defects. All of these changes create windows of increased risk for stroke if not enough medication is given and for life-threatening hemorrhage if too much medication is administered. Furthermore, any procedure, in truth even brushing her teeth, places her at risk for endocarditis. We have antibiotic protocols, but they are imperfect too.

Of course, even more perilous is any subsequent pregnancy. *If I do the surgery and she subsequently gets pregnant and dies either directly or indirectly because of the pregnancy, what responsibility would I carry for her death?*

I offer her counseling to explore why she is willing to take such serious risks to have a child.

Desta counters that I am imposing my values on her. She certainly values her life. But it is her right to decide what risks to take for herself and any potential child. Without question, no one would refuse her care if she got pregnant on her own. Furthermore, if I did the surgery, I would not be getting her pregnant, only returning her body to its normal state. She would bear all the responsibility for getting pregnant.

I believe strongly in patient autonomy. A colleague once asked why so many Jewish doctors were pro-choice. I explained we highly value patient autonomy, a natural outgrowth of constantly being the minority in society.

The medical world does not deny patients care because they made poor choices. My broken leg was fixed when I skied too fast. The drunk driver in a lethal motor vehicle accident gets care. Our tax dollars pay for the ravages of smoking, obesity, and inadequate exercise. Desta did not get Asherman's syndrome by choice. One could even argue that the medical world may have caused it with the D&C.

Perfectly healthy patients can have devastating outcomes in pregnancy, both for the mother and for the baby. In fact, it is much safer to have an abortion than to continue a pregnancy. Adults have a right to reproduce. My mind reviews some of the cases that have stressed my autonomy creed. There are the two quadriplegics at the university infertility clinic trying to conceive. There are the multitudes of women who weigh more than 350 pounds, have diabetes and hypertension, and are at this moment getting pregnant in the infertility clinic three floors above mine. And there were patients with HIV or even AIDS intentionally getting pregnant in the late 1980s when the transmission risk to the baby was 30 percent, and their own life expectancy was short.

Perinatal physicians (high-risk obstetricians) in my community routinely care for patients as risky and complicated as Desta. Our neonatal intensive care unit (NICU) is among the best in the world, with micropremies—babies born at little more than halfway through the forty weeks of pregnancy—surviving and thriving. Desta is very clear that she is willing to die to get a child far enough along in gestation to survive, even if it means that the child will face serious challenges due to prematurity and/or losing his or her mother.

I look at my hands. It is not unreasonable to surgically correct her Asherman's. I have the know-how, training, and setting to do it relatively safely. Desta cannot do it for herself. As a member of the medical community, do I have an obligation to restore Desta's uterus to a relatively normal state? I know I am obligated to return "lost property," (Deuteronomy 22:2); I see myself as morally obligated to heal people. These are expressions of *tikkun olam,* a way to be God's partner in the ongoing act of creation. But the sole purpose of the surgery in her mind is to get her pregnant, a much more life-threatening condition for her than it normally is for most women. What would God want me to do?

Who am I to judge what is right for her? I believe she clearly understands the risks of pregnancy to herself and her potential child. In general, I like to think of myself as a guide to the complex medical world for my patients. For me, "Love your neighbor as yourself" means respecting an individual's desires, hopes, and dreams, even if they differ from my own. In the end, a patient gets to decide for herself if she wants a treatment or therapy. A patient can choose surgery and chemotherapy or just let the cancer take its course. Although it would cause me great pain (and I spend hours with patients in an effort to avoid the poor communication of which this scenario is a ramification), I would never force a nondelusional woman to have a cesarean section to save her baby, because her body is her own.

I speak with colleagues, friends, parents, a rabbi, the head of the hospital ethics committee, and a philosophy professor. The last of those would do the surgery if he were me; most of the rest are somewhere on the fence. Some would say no. A close friend's mother is the most succinct, saying "Oy, why would you want that on your *kup?*" It makes me realize I have been thinking so much about Desta that I have not thought about myself. If she gets pregnant and dies, I will feel my surgical actions aided and abetted her death. Although it would be with her permission and blessing—even fulfilling her greatest hope—I will know I hastened her death. In medical ethics the rule is nonmaleficence, "first do no harm." Even though harm is far from guaranteed in this case, the risk is high enough that I believe by refusing to do the surgery I am protecting her life. Judaism clearly mandates the protection of life over nearly all other commandments, based on the rabbis' interpretation of Leviticus 18:5.

I tell Desta I will not do the surgery. I have also been unable to find a colleague in our metropolitan area willing to do it. Her face falls. She is crushed. My heart aches for her. We both cry. Rabbi Akiva's classic scenario with the water and two men in the desert does not fit from where either one of us stand. I see her life versus a life that does not yet exist and hence cannot be snuffed out. Of course she gets the water. But she can already see her not-yet-conceived son or daughter and, like any mother, will of course give the water to her child.

Nearly ten years have passed since this encounter. I see Desta at least once a year. She finds it painful to come to my office because it is a reminder of her infertility. Her affect is sad, despite antidepressants. Her overall presence is much diminished from the person I first met. She fills even less space than her current 92 pounds would suggest. She is now disabled. Her heart failure has progressed so much that she cannot walk ten yards without stopping to catch her breath. Her mother died recently in Ethiopia, but Desta was too ill to contemplate traveling there to say good-bye. Desta is still married.

I stole possibility, hope, and dreams by saying no. Those too are a part of being made in God's image, hence a part of what I am charged with caretaking. I still wonder if I did the right thing.

Helping the Healer of Israel: Perspectives of a Jewish Physician

Robert S. Karasov

"DOCTOR, MY son is an above-average student, but he has always had problems concentrating and sitting still. The SATs are in a few months, and I really think he has attention deficit disorder like my older son. I want him to do his best and would like to try him on Ritalin." As a pediatrician who specializes in psychopharmacology, I am often confronted with such scenarios. How am I to deal with these issues? What values do I need to balance to determine the correct response to patients with mental health concerns?

Judaism values caring for one's body. We are forbidden from doing anything to intentionally harm the body, such as abusing drugs. We are also taught that we are made in God's image and the body is a holy vessel that houses the soul. Every morning, during the morning prayers, we thank God for fashioning our bodies with wisdom, remembering its precise balance of organs and functions. And at *brit milah* ceremonies, we are reminded that the circumcised male is considered the perfect physical state. This implies that the goal of actively seeking perfection for the human body is a Jewish religious goal.

Other teachings lead to different goals. Judaism encourages us to push ourselves to succeed in a variety of ways. We should fill the earth and have dominion over it. We should try to master a broad range of Jewish and secular learning. Our *yetzer ha-rah,* "evil inclination," is seen as a necessary force to motivate us and help us fulfill our purpose on earth.

What happens when values such as these come into conflict? When our bodies are not functioning as perfectly as we would like, we lose some of our abilities to accomplish physically or mentally all that we are capable of. Judaism values medicine and encourages people actively to seek medical treatments. Our ability to understand the inner workings of the body and make medical advances is seen as a further way of honoring God and using the intellect that God gave us. To be a healer is to imitate God, who is the ultimate healer. So far so good. No apparent conflict. However, what happens when people start trying to maximize their performance, not to treat a disease but to give themselves an edge by using performance-enhancing steroids? Most people would agree that this is

86

wrong because it is dangerous and "cheating" as it relates to athletic competition. But what if you used these "treatments" in order to succeed at your job, a job you needed to provide for your family? Would family duties justify these actions? Would they be in accordance with Jewish law? What about someone who is naturally short and has low self-esteem or suffers mental anguish because of his height? Is it appropriate to give him growth hormone even if he is not deficient in this hormone? Is this using our intellect to imitate God's abilities?

One area that has received much publicity is the use of prescription medications for treatment of attention deficit disorder, depression, anxiety, sleep disorders, and many other mental health diagnoses. Certain cases are clear-cut. Everyone, except the most virulently antimedication extremists, would agree that patients who are suicidal or nonfunctional because of severe symptoms should receive medication to improve their functioning and restore them to health. On the other end of the spectrum are patients who are abusing prescription drugs to avoid dealing with life's problems—for example, compulsively driven people chronically using stimulant drugs to deal with inadequate sleep or chronically overwhelmed patients using antianxiety meds that keep them in a perpetual stupor. Most would agree that this is wrong from both a medical and a Jewish perspective. However, what about cases less clear-cut, such as the one I outlined at the start of the essay?

Attention deficit hyperactivity disorder (ADHD) is a very imprecise diagnosis. It is arbitrarily defined as the lowest 5 percent of the population in ability to pay attention or control impulsivity or hyperactivity, leading to functional impairment. But many parents, especially the many high achievers in the Jewish community, are not content to be told their child does not have a problem, if he or she is in the lowest 10 percent. Is a child who receives Bs and Cs or even As and Bs considered "functionally impaired" if he or she is bright enough to do better? In addition, despite negative publicity to the contrary, stimulant medications like Ritalin have been studied more than any other class of drugs and have been found to be extremely effective with minimal long-term risks. Is my denial of medication to a student with moderately weak attention skills imposing my values on the family? Is my giving medication not doing the same? How many of us use caffeine to enhance our performance? Is there a difference? There are no clear answers to these questions.

Jennifer, age 12, gets nervous at night before tests or performances and takes an hour to fall asleep. She requests the same sleeping pills her father takes. Eight-year-old Jacob's father died of cancer one month ago. Jacob still cries several times per week and has been reluctant to attend several activities. His mother requests antidepressants for him. What should I do? Can Judaism's understanding of the role of suffering help me with my patients? Many patients ask for medication seeking perfect lives, free of physical or mental pain or blemishes. Is this appropriate? Is there a value in suffering? In general, Judaism does not extol the virtues of suffering. However, in the stories of the patriarchs we certainly see examples of emotional growth that comes through hardship and pain, grief or disappointment. Perhaps the clearest example is Judah. His emotional growth following the death of two sons prepared him to speak eloquently and soulfully to Joseph as he pleaded for the release of his brother Benjamin (Genesis 44:18).

Pain leads to growth. Judaism offers several models of this. Jewish laws of mourning are designed to help people cope naturally with life's pain and emerge with stronger community and family bonds. Fasting is described as "afflicting one's soul" (Numbers 29:7), and on Yom Kippur this is one way we try to get closer to God. The older I get, the more I can look back on painful experiences in my own life and see how profoundly they have positively shaped who I am today. The expression "what doesn't kill you will make you stronger" is very apt. Do medications that blunt emotions also blunt the emotional growth that should occur? I do not think there are answers to this question. Judaism sees everything in life, both the good and the bad, as coming from God. To me this implies that we should try to live through all of life's experiences as consciously as possible, without medications that numb us to the outside world. Judaism is all about balance. The pursuit of perfect, pain-free lives is not the work for which we were created. It is to struggle, grow, appreciate the beauty of life, and—in the process—become closer to God. Jennifer and Jacob need time, nurturing, and emotional support more than they need medication.

I have been seeing the Johnson kids since they were each born. The family seemed happy and intact until, at Tim's fourteen-year checkup, Mrs. Johnson informed me that her husband left her suddenly four months earlier. She was devastated, and Tim was also not handling it well. He was sullen and angry, and his grades were plummeting. He did not want to see his friends and spent hours alone in his room. Tim told me he sometimes wished he were dead. His mother recently started Prozac, which has helped her cope, and she wonders if Tim might also benefit from medication. Tim was clearly depressed and in great psychic pain. His symptoms have not been improving. Is medication the answer? Shouldn't I do what I can to relieve Tim's pain? Is Tim strong enough, with love and support, to work through his grief without medication, or will he fall into the abyss that can lead to devastating adolescent problems or even suicide? We discussed medication, and I referred Tim to a psychologist. I asked his mom to identify other adult men in his life that can help support him, and I tried to help Tim focus on what he has to live for. I will see him again in a few weeks to reassess how he is doing. Clearly, there are times when life's pain is more than we can handle and medication is appropriate. With preteens, it is even more complicated. These children do not generally benefit from counseling; and medications for depression do not work very well, if at all, and are not as safe as the medications for ADHD. However, every child responds differently, so if a child is in enough pain, I still often try medication.

Making predictions about how much inner strength a child has is very difficult. When I am feeling unsure about a decision, I take comfort in my belief that our sense of control over our own lives is really an illusion. One sentence in the *Amidah* has given me more comfort than any other. It is found in the *Modim Anachnu Lakh* paragraph and reads in part, "We thank you God . . . for our lives. which are in your hands . . . [and] for your miracles that are with us every day." God is the healer of Israel and all humankind. As physicians, we are merely God's helpers. All of our actions have so many unintended and unforeseen consequences, both positive and negative, that we have to be humble about our role in helping our patients. Somehow, patients recover, relationships are repaired, and people find renewed meaning in life. These are all daily miracles. This attitude should not be confused with passivity. Judaism is very clear about not relying on miracles. However, it does give me more peace of mind and optimism for my patients.

Claire, age 17, who has a long-standing history of mood disorder, attention deficit disorder, and oppositional disorder, came to see me with her mother and her court-appointed guardian *ad litum* for a second opinion. Her parents had an extremely contentious divorce and have had ongoing custody battles for three years, with Claire preferring to live first with one parent then the other. She has had truancy issues and lived briefly in a group home. She has explosive outbursts of anger that are causing severe problems at home and school. She feels she has nothing to live for. Claire has tried several medications. She is currently taking lithium, which works the best for her, but she refuses blood draws to monitor for lithium toxicity, and so we have no idea whether she is on an adequate dose. When I entered the room, she was slouched down in her chair with her arms crossed glaring at the floor.

Claire's life is falling apart around her. Her parents, who also have mental health and drug problems, are unable to control her or provide a stable environment. She clearly needs medication. But how much risk should I expose Claire to by using the potentially toxic drug lithium without proper blood monitoring? How much should I expose myself to malpractice claims by using lithium without adequate monitoring? I decided to reduce the dose of lithium and try other safer medicines first. Unfortunately, nothing else worked well, and Claire continued to deteriorate. I increased the lithium again to her old dose, and she improved to her prior dysfunctional level.

Claire's case is all about balancing risks. What are the risks of treating versus the risks of not treating or undertreating? Untreated, Claire is at risk for loss of self-esteem, school failure, drug abuse, pregnancy, sexually transmitted diseases, and suicide. On the other hand, lithium can cause thyroid and kidney problems if blood levels are too high. How do I decide?

Judaism supports patient autonomy. A patient is allowed to choose among various treatments or decline treatment if he or she thinks it will be too painful. However, if there is risk of death and a good treatment exists, patients must seek that treatment. In Claire's case the very mental illness that was making her decline blood draws was what needed treatment. Claire and her family were so overwhelmed by her crisis that they could not really balance the long-term risks against the benefits of short-term improvement. I felt that I needed to put myself in the parents' place and make a decision of what was overall in Claire's best interests. I knew the family trusted me to use my judgment and decide for them. How high could I push the dose without monitoring? Jewish law does allow us to undergo risky experimental treatments if the risk of not treating is great and there are no other acceptable alternatives. Depending on how bad Claire's crisis became, I may have needed to blindly push the dose higher. If she suffered kidney or thyroid problems, I could have been charged with malpractice. Judaism does not require me to put myself in any danger to save another person, but it does encourage me to take reasonable risks. At our last visit, I again explained that higher doses would really help, but we needed blood levels. She tentatively agreed.

What patients desire most is to feel heard and know we care about them. It is hard to predict what influences we will have on our patients' lives. Recall the man Joseph encountered when he was searching for his brothers. The man told Joseph where to find his brothers, information that led to Joseph's sale into slavery (Genesis 37:15). Without this anonymous messenger, Jewish history would be very different. The rabbis say this man was a *malakh*. However the Hebrew word *malakh* is ambiguous. It means "angel" and also "human messenger." Being in the right place at the right time can allow us to be messengers of God without even realizing it. I believe we are all *malakhim* at times in our lives. And, like Joseph's *malakh*, we do not always know the significance of our actions.

Medical decisions are never made in a vacuum. They are very dependent on trust and the strength of the doctor–patient relationship. Patients worry that doctors are denying them treatment to save money or that the doctor does not truly understand their situation. Sometimes they are right. Doctors often need to meet patients halfway between the patients' demands and current medical recommendations. This may mean short-term use of medications or referrals or tests that the doctor feels are unnecessary but that the patients feel they need. The goal is to build trust and educate the patient so he or she will have confidence in future recommendations.

Judaism recognizes the need for gradual changes in behavior. The book of Exodus is all about the gradual transition needed to transform an enslaved people into a nation. Not even an event like Sinai could lead to rapid, radical change. We see a similar dynamic when potential converts to Judaism consult rabbis about commandments or beliefs they do not feel ready to take on. Rabbis meet people where they are, educate them and move them toward the goal of fuller acceptance of Judaism. If rabbis do not see adequate growth, they may ultimately turn down the person's request to convert. Likewise, sometimes a doctor does not see attitude changes in a patient that would lead to a healthier balance between demands for medications and making lifestyle changes; or sometimes there is persistent lack of trust in the relationship. At times, if philosophical differences are too great, doctors must even end the relationship. Thankfully, this is a rare occurrence. The values that go into making most day-to-day medical decisions are rarely consciously articulated. However, I believe that the Jewish values I discussed in this essay, as well as many other Jewish values, shape who I am as a person and as a physician. Being aware of these values helps me recognize that many of my medical decisions are not completely objective, and physicians with other values may come to different, but equally valid decisions. It is part of what continues to make medicine an art.

Jews and Tattoos

Kosher Ink: The Emerging World of Tattooed Jews

Andy Abrams

W HEN I was a boy, the only Jewish people I knew with tattoos were Holocaust survivors. The faded numbers inked on their arms, their immigrant accents, the Yiddish they spoke together—this left a mark on my identity as indelible as any tattoo. Those numbers were a reminder of a painful tragedy reflected in a symbol of hate and genocide. Seeing tattoos from the Holocaust was also a testament to survival and a poignant reminder of a history of persecution. Tattooed Jews of my grandparents' generation served as a deterrent against getting tattooed for me and many other contemporary Jews.

However, when I spotted my first Hebrew tattoo several years ago, it sparked my intense interest. I spent the last four years working on the film and book project *Tattoo Jew.* I have conducted interviews, compiled research, filmed, written, and lectured on this topic. This placed me in a unique position as a primary source on the emerging culture of tattooed Jews.

For a Jewish person, getting a Jewish tattoo is an act rooted in conflict. There is the disapproval of family and community, there are the religious prohibitions, and there is the powerful deterrent of the Holocaust as a cultural memory. Most of the people choosing to get tattoos, particularly tattoos with Jewish themes and images, are under the age of thirty-five. Most people over the age of fifty are profoundly resistant to the idea of Jews with tattoos, regardless of their level of religious observance. There is a rift about tattoos that is deeper and more dramatic than on any other issue. My work is dedicated to examining tattoos in a Jewish context. I also explore the desire to connect to Jewish identity through tattoo art that is unique and often beautiful, but still highly controversial in the Jewish community.

The Judaic view on this issue is simple: Jewish people are not allowed to have tattoos. It is forbidden. The Torah prohibits tattooing where it states, "You shall not mark your flesh for the dead, nor incise any marks on yourselves: I am the LORD" (Leviticus 19:28). In addition, it is written that "You shall not cut yourselves," (Deuteronomy. 14:1), which many rabbis have interpreted to include tattooing. Aside from the general prohibition, the subsequent commentaries and historical record offer conflicting viewpoints about the exact nature and specifics of the injunction against tattoos. An anonymous author says, "If a man writes on his skin, he is culpable, but only if it leaves a permanent mark" (Mishnah, Makkot 3:6); however, the very same source goes on to add a contrary view from Rabbi Simeon ben Judah, who says, "He is not culpable unless he writes the name of God, for it is written, 'nor incise any marks on yourselves: I am the Lord.'" This demonstrates an existing debate about the interpretation of the accepted prohibition against tattooing in Leviticus. I argue that the reference in Leviticus is tied to the burial practices of various pagan societies, which concurs with the view stated by Maimonides, that "this was a custom among the pagans who marked themselves for idolatry" (*Hilkhot Avodat Kokhavim* 12:11). However, there are clear examples of Judaic tattooing during biblical times. One reference says, "One shall say 'I am the Lord's,' another shall use the name of Jacob, another shall mark his arm 'of the Lord's,' and adopt the name of Israel" (Isaiah 44:5). Following, it says, "See, I have engraved you on the palms of my hands" (Isaiah 49:16).

The widely accepted viewpoint that tattoos are not for Jews is deeply entrenched but misguided. There was a history of tattooing in Judaism according to several biblical scholars, and the texts themselves are not as clear as many people believe. The prohibition is open to interpretation, and Judaism is not a stagnant thing. We change and evolve with the times.

I suggest, therefore, that the law be interpreted to allow tattoos within certain limits. For example, I believe in prohibiting negative tattoos such as those that depict violence or nudity. I think it is also reasonable to ban tattoos of God's name. However, I feel strongly that we should allow tattoos that illustrate Jewish themes or other healthy images such as flowers, natural scenes, and animals.

If the religious prohibition itself is not enough to keep young Jews from getting inked, there is a very popular myth that is familiar to most people. It is said that a Jewish person with a tattoo may not be buried in a Jewish cemetery. In fact, this is not true at all, as any person familiar with Jewish law can tell you. However, it has been repeated so many times that many people believe it to be a fact that they will not be welcome in a Jewish cemetery with their ink. One unexpected outcome of my work has been to debunk this misconception.

Beyond the religious prohibition, and the mistaken fear of being banned from burial in a Jewish cemetery, it is the memory of the Holocaust that has exerted the most powerful influence on the decision of many young people who are considering a tattoo. Everyone has seen old black-and-white photographs of pale and emaciated survivors at the concentration camps. The image of numbers tattooed on the arms of Jews is imprinted in the minds of Jews everywhere. The Holocaust conjures familiar images of pain and suffering. People know the stories of death camps, and they have seen photographs of trains taking Jews to their slaughter. Just some sixty years ago the Nazis killed six million Jews. The survivors have told the tales of brutality, cruelty, and mass murder. At Auschwitz, they stood in the mud, naked under gray skies. Tattoo needles buzzed as they were robbed of their individuality, marked with numbers as if they were cattle being branded. They were tattooed with those numbers as a way of dehumanizing them.

Because Jews were forcibly marked with numbers, the idea of Jewish tattoos often causes controversy in the Jewish community. For many people it is a reminder of a past that is too painful. Moreover, many parents of Jews tattooed with Jewish symbols fear for the safety of their children, feeling that they are at risk by having tattoos that call attention to their Jewish identity.

Anti-Semitism is very real, and parents' concern for the safety of their children should not be taken lightly. Many of the interview subjects in *Tattoo Jew* articulated a response to this issue directly through their tattoos. All of the people I have interviewed who have tattoos with Jewish themes get those tattoos for similar reasons; each of them wants to wear their Jewishness proudly on their skin. It is a way for them to mark themselves as Jews in an act of pride. According to Orian Livnat, a tattooed Israeli-American who has lived in the United States for most of his life, "You have to stand up for yourself. This is a way for me to show the world I am not afraid. I'm proud to be Jewish."

In one dramatic case, a woman named Marina Vainshtein has dedicated her entire body to be tattooed with images of the Holocaust. "They were humiliated, treated like animals, and then they were killed—six million Jews dead," Marina said. She has made it her mission in life to make sure that the world never forgets the atrocity of the Holocaust, a topic about which she feels passionate. "They removed all humanity from them. Jews became a number instead of being a person," she said. "They degraded them with tattoos, and dehumanized them as individuals." What she wears on her skin is a memorial to all of the lives that were lost under the fascist regime of the Third Reich. "For me it is a way to reclaim something," Marina told me, "It is a political act and it is a bold statement to have these tattoos. I want people to remember what happened there. It's something so important to me that I've made my skin a canvas dedicated to remembering the Holocaust."

Marina's tattoos are not for the faint of heart. Her tattoo art is compromised of black ink and shading work only, and includes an elaborate back piece that features a skeletal angel sitting on a coffin weeping, a train driving to Auschwitz, the open doors to an oven like the ones the Nazis used to burn Jews, a field of gravestones, and a scene of a death camp being liberated. Marina has words in Hebrew across her shoulders that translate into English as "The Earth Hide Not My Blood," taken from a book of art by Holocaust survivors. On her lower back is a Star of David in flames under which are the words in Hebrew, *lo tishkah,* meaning "never forget." She has a number surrounded by flames tattooed on her forearm. On her stomach there is a synagogue on fire and an image of a lamp made from human skin. Across Marina's chest, in English, are the words "Never Again" in stylized script.

Although the tattooed Jewish community is in its infancy, there is a developing synthesis of Judaic concepts, Hebrew, and Jewish-centric symbols with some of the more traditional iconography of tattooing. I have been photographing and interviewing unique people who are starting to blend traditional tattoo images with concepts from their Jewish identity. All of Orian Livnat's tattoos use familiar tattoo images and at the same time they relate to his Jewishness. The words in his tattoos are done in Hebrew. "On my left arm there is a background of Japanese-style clouds and cherry blossoms interwoven with the image of the world on fire in blue flames, and *chai,* the Hebrew word "life," is written in the center of the world," Orian told me. On his right arm there is a rose with six drops of blood. "One drop of blood for every million Jews killed in the Holocaust," he said. Under the rose is a gravestone with a Star of David sitting above a flaming skull and crossbones and the Hebrew word *zakhor,* which means "remember." Next to the tombstone is a dove designed in the traditional style of a tattooed bluebird; it is stabbed through with a long dagger; a banner next to it reads "Tragedy." On his elaborate chest piece, with cherubic angels and the words *imma* and *abba,* meaning "mother" and "father," written on a banner in Hebrew, there is a Star of

David designed like a nautical star (a five-pointed star historically tattooed on sailors, characterized by each point being divided half in black and half in color). Orian has found a creative way to join the worlds of traditional Judaism and tattoo culture seamlessly.

Times are changing, and Judaism will, I hope, adapt to this emerging trend. Even though tattoos are forbidden under religious law, there are many Jewish people who are beginning to make connections between their tattoo work and their spirituality. In some ways it appears that Jewish people are choosing Jewish tattoos as a new form of ritual identification, a new way to embrace and cement their identity and spirituality. While it may not be popular among religious traditionalists, what interview subjects say is that their Jewish tattoos are as important to them as any Jewish rituals in their lives. I am not suggesting that tattoos will replace the *bris* or the bar mitzvah, but there is a significant movement to use tattoos as a supplemental, personal ritual. I often explain the prevalence of Jewish-themed tattoos as being a unique combination of a bar mitzvah and wearing a yarmulke; it serves to deepen a personal connection with Jewish identity while marking oneself publicly as a Jew. According to Dylan Weiswasser, "My tattoos do not keep me from connecting with God—it's the opposite. I pray every day because if I don't, I feel vexed inside. I say a prayer for protection, and I ask the Lord to be my strength and shield as he was with King David. My ink is my covenant with myself, and I think God would approve. Plus, the Star of David on my elbow always reminds me that the world is judging me for being Jewish."

Tattoos demonstrate an identity that is permanently etched in ink. The interview subjects in *Tattoo Jew* are finding new ways of expressing their Jewish pride. They are using their tattoos to reinforce their Judaism and are deeply connected to their Jewish roots. Although they may see themselves as outsiders in parts of the Jewish community, their tattoos express a desire for belonging. It is a statement for a Jewish person to get inked with words and symbols expressing Jewish heritage. This is a profound metaphorical act with deep resonance. These tattoos are dramatic, often purposefully so. They carry the heavy weight of Jewish culture, history, and religion in ways that even tattooed Jews themselves find surprising. This new and growing expression of Jewishness is an act of defiance and yet also an act of pride.

There is a growing trend of Jewish people, one that explores a new Jewish identity, written or expressed as artistic and symbolic pieces drawn directly on the body. We are known as the People of the Book, a fact taken literally by tattooed Jews. They are wearing their Judaism on their skin in visually stunning tattoo art. They are writing the modern history of their Judaic selves on their own skin. By examining seemingly extreme behavior on the margins of Jewish culture, we stand to learn a great deal about what it means to be Jewish. Through *Tattoo Jew* I am exposing an emerging expression of Jewishness, which speaks directly to the culture and experience of a younger generation. This is a study of the complexities of the individual in relation to religious law, the struggle against assimilation, and the desire to maintain a strong Jewish self. The Jewish community can benefit as a whole by seeing this trend as one of the many ways we define who we are and how we choose to express our identity to the world.

Lynn's Tattoo

Rebecca T. Alpert

WHEN MY daughter, Lynn, was growing up, she never expressed an interest in getting a tattoo; in fact she seemed to think the pain could not possibly be worth it. When it came to issues about her body, I made what seemed to both of us a fair rule; put anything you want "on" your body (hair, nails, piercings, clothing), but be very careful about what you put "in" your body (tobacco, drugs, alcohol, too much or too little food, other people's body parts). We tangled about this only once, and that was when she wanted me to take her to pierce her navel for a Bat Mitzvah present. I told her I was not ready to do that, but that if she still wanted that as a gift when she was 16, I would agree. She did, and I did. It was an important experience for both of us that taught us about patience and keeping promises.

When Lynn was 21, her thoughts about getting a tattoo changed, and she began to entertain ideas about the images or words with which she might like to express herself and where on her body she might want to put them. I would not at that point have tried to advise or forbid her; she was an adult and would make her own decisions; and unless she asked for my advice, I tried my best not to give any. I had every reason to assume that things I might worry about as a parent, like matters of safety and health, would be choices she would make well.

But whatever comfort that gave me, I had to face the fact that tattoos were not very appealing to me in general. When I was growing up, tattoos were for sailors and motor bike guys; "proper" people just did not do that sort of thing, and for women and Jews it was unheard of. I gave some thought to my own feelings, just to make sure I understood them. Was this dislike of tattoos based on values that were important to me or was it a prejudice against something I thought was inappropriate for "people like me" based on stereotypes I had about the kind of people I associated with tattooing? Was I simply uncomfortable with the idea that my daughter would willingly experience pain to do this? Was I troubled by the idea she would be doing something that would alter her permanently? It was already clear that it would affect her career choices, as at least one of the art teachers for whom she was modeling told her that they could no longer use her to pose. And tattoos fail the easy in/on distinction that I made on other subjects as she was growing up, since while they appear on the skin's surface, they also penetrate beneath it.

99

I needed a better way to understand this problem for myself, so I did what I often do: I looked for Jewish wisdom on the subject. I do not believe ethical decisions can be made in isolation or based only on your own intuitions or gut reactions. I wanted to test my ideas and feelings, and I wanted help thinking them through. As a Reconstructionist rabbi, I use the tradition in the way my teacher Mordecai Kaplan taught me to do. I start with what is in the Bible and Talmud because it is my heritage. I may not always follow the letter of the law; in fact, I often find myself at odds with what I find there. But to me, being a good Jew means being in conversation with the tradition, and what I find in these texts is helpful for clarifying my own position, even if it is only something to argue against. I also believe that Jewish law is flexible and changes over time, that it is always susceptible to new interpretations, inviting dialogue and discussion. As part of this process, I may also look to other sources, including ones from other traditions, putting them alongside my own thoughts into conversation with what I find in my heritage. The process always works when I need to decide something or form some opinion, and I am never sure of the results before hand, which also makes it exciting to do.

As I began to consider this question, I thought immediately of the powerful story of Rabbi Meir and his wife, Beruriah, whose twin sons died on the Sabbath. Beruriah kept the news from Meir until the Sabbath was over, and then she told him a parable. She asked him what he would do if he had gotten a precious gift and the original owner wanted it back. Meir agreed that he would return the gift, of course. Only then did she tell him about the loss of their sons. The story is meant to make it clear to us that God only lends us our bodies as a precious gift for a period of time, and we must give them back to the source from which they came, perhaps with sadness, but always aware that our bodies are not our own; we have them only for a time, and we are their caretakers, not their owners. Because our bodies are a gift from God and do not belong to us, the rabbis teach that we must not do anything to our bodies that would harm them.

I wondered if tattooing would fall under the category of harming our bodies that the tradition cautions against. Things like smoking, excessive drinking, failure to exercise, and failure to eat properly have all been considered the kinds of abuse we are not permitted to do to our bodies. Jews have also refused to have autopsies performed, donate our bodies to science, or to cremate our bodies, because we are supposed to leave them in the form in which they came. In recent years, however, some of these rules have been relaxed because, for example, organ donation now clearly can save someone's life, and saving a life is a higher value than preserving and honoring our bodies. Alterations that are for health or safety (like the amputation of a limb or tattooing that is necessary for radiation therapy) are, of course, also permitted because of how much we value saving human life.

But is tattooing harming your body at all? To my daughter and many, many other young people today, abusing a gift from God is the last thing on their minds. They would consider tattoos a kind of *hiddur mitzvah,* a way to enhance the commandment to honor our bodies, by making them more beautiful and therefore in keeping with Jewish values about our obligation as humans to make things in this world, including ourselves, more beautiful

I gave much thought to this argument, and realized that for Lynn, as for most people, the tattoo she decided to get (an art nouveau design based on ornamentation of a building by the architect Victor Horta, the Hotel Tassel in Brussels, 1893–1897) made her body beautiful. As she explained it to me:

> About my tattoo . . . aesthetics are very important to me, as someone who is very interested in art, architecture, design, and decoration. The ability to decorate my own body, therefore, is an interesting idea. The tattoo is based on the interior design of my favorite build-ing in the world. As something that I have studied and visited, it is very close to my heart and represents a part of who I am and what inspires me. The ability to be able to take this thing that I find abso-lutely perfectly beautiful and make it a part of my own body is what made me want to get a tattoo. I think it enhances or decorates my body in an interesting way while also being a very personal, mean-ingful, and inspirational part of my life.

I had to accept the fact that her way of enhancing herself was probably more in keeping with Jewish tradition than my own. Although Judaism preaches about *tzeniut* (modesty) and suggests that women's bodies should be covered up, the Jewish community also encourages women to dress stylishly; wear makeup and jewelry; and emphasize femininity by not wearing "men's clothing," especially to synagogue and especially on the Sabbath. One of the reasons my working-class mother never wanted to join a synagogue was because she was afraid she might be embarrassed by her lack of expensive clothing. If anything, my daughter's tattoo is more appropriately Jewish by these standards than my tendencies to dress in the 1970s lesbian feminist tradition that I am fond of; I would wear jeans and T-shirts all the time if I could, and I would wear makeup only when I had to do so. As much as I hate dressing up and shopping for clothes, my daughter loves style and fashion. Her tattoo is part of that, and it is a difference between us that I have learned to respect.

But there is more to tattoos and the Jews than rethinking the meaning of one Jewish value, even a central one. Type "Judaism and Tattoos" into Google, and you will find a very different conversation from the one I had with myself and my daughter on the subject. If you do this search, you will be quite overwhelmed by the vast number of sites where this topic is discussed in depth and at length. Searching through these websites, you can discover opinions by all kinds of Jews: American and Israeli; Orthodox, Conservative, Reconstructionist, Reform, and secular; young and old (but mostly young); rabbis and tattoo artists, filmmakers, journalists, and bloggers. Mostly there are stories about how Judaism factors into decisions young Jews are making about getting tattooed. There is also a site for the documentary film that is now being made, *Tattoo Jews,* that features interviews with Jews who have tattoos in the San Francisco Bay area (www.tattoojewmovie.com). And then there is "Tattoos Are Not for Jews" by Israeli activist Michael Lerner, who is credited with getting the state of Israel to pass a law requiring parental permission for tattooing under age children[1] (www.geocities.com/mnlerner2000). By my parenting standards, that is a good idea anyway. In any case, it is no surprise that there is much passionate argument on the topic. Yet, it is amazing that almost all of the sites touch on three key points.

First, the Hebrew Bible has a definitive statement on the subject, found in Leviticus 19:28, "You shall not make gashes in your flesh for the dead, or incise any marks on yourselves: I am the LORD." But while the statement may be definitive, its meaning is open to interpretation, even among the most traditional writers.

---

1. See Louis E. Newman, "Ethics, Faith and Healing: Jewish Physicians Reflect on Medical Practice," in *Caring Well: Religion, Narrative and Health Care Ethics,* edited by David H. Smith (Louisville, KY: Westminster John Knox Press, 2000), 117–143.

Second, even though "everyone" thinks that having a tattoo means that you may not be buried in a Jewish cemetery, that is just not the case. And while no one seems to know how this idea became so widely known and assumed to be true, all the websites want to make sure everyone knows that although tattooing is against Jewish law it would not prohibit burial in a Jewish cemetery any more than not keeping kosher would.

Third, the meaning of tattooing for Jews cannot be separated from the numbers the Nazis tattooed on the arms of Jewish men and women in Auschwitz and other camps during the Holocaust in an effort to categorize and thereby dehumanize them.

Did anything I learned from these conversations change my perspective? The biblical prohibition made me aware that tattooing is an ancient practice and oddly enough increased my respect for it. I presume that the first part (about "not making gashes . . . for the dead") has to do with keeping the Israelites from copying funeral rituals that were performed by the tribes and groups that lived in the land of Canaan and, therefore, is not relevant to contemporary conversations about tattooing for beautification. The rule against "incising any marks on yourselves" was another matter, a clear prohibition. But as a Jew who does not follow most of the rules in the Torah (from doing certain kinds of work on the Sabbath, to mixing linen and wool together in my clothing), I am not sure that this one would change my mind.

As for being buried in a Jewish cemetery, I am glad that the people who write on the Internet are trying to clear up this misconception. I checked this out with my (untattooed) son who just returned from a trip to Israel. To my surprise, not only did this topic come up in conversation but all the American Jews he met did believe that getting tattooed would prohibit their burial in a Jewish cemetery, although this idea really shocked the Israelis among them. Although this has no bearing on my daughter's situation, it is one of the most interesting things I learned about in this process. I really wonder how urban legends like these get started and how they take on so much power. I am also touched (and a bit confused) about why burial would matter so much to these young Jews.

So what to do about the Holocaust? In my mind I return to an exhibit I saw in Vienna last summer in the small Jewish museum there of a series of photographs of tattooed arms of survivors from Auschwitz. There were at least 100 of them. Each photograph was the same on the surface, and yet each one was completely different—jewelry, watches, skin tones all reflecting the individuality of the anonymous survivor—in spite of all efforts to make them disappear. The exhibit was powerful; a reminder that there are some things that cannot be erased, that need to be seen to be believed, and that Jews choosing to make their bodies into art may support in its own way.

Mostly, I was deeply touched by all the stories on these websites of young Jews seeking Jewish identification and finding it through their tattoos. The fact that many young people now have tattoos, are thinking about what that means for them in terms of their Jewish identities, and are even decorating themselves with Jewish images and themes, can only be good for the Jews. In fact, my daughter writes:

> I wanted to get my Hebrew name tattooed on my wrist because it is also something that means a lot to me, is a deep part of me. I have hesitated in getting it done because aesthetics are also very important to me and I am not sure that I would be happy with how it looks on my body. Those are the two main parts of the decision-making process for me: what is an image that means something intensely important to me and my identity, and then what will it look like as a part of my physical appearance for the rest of my life?

I was thrilled to know that Lynn's Jewish identity means so much to her that she would want to wear it around in public every day, since she is not interested in other Jewish religious practice or communal connections. But that she would think about marking Hebrew indelibly on her body "as a sign on her hand" is a powerful statement to me of her connection to being Jewish, one that I can honestly say I celebrate.

PART III

&

CONCLUSION

Our Bodies, Our Selves, Our Values

W E ARE all embodied creatures. Our lives, our sense of self, and our experience of the world—all are shaped in myriad ways by the fact that we have bodies. This much is certain, whatever else we may believe about the things that define us as human beings. Our personalities, our spirits or souls, our imagination, and our thought processes—all the parts of ourselves that we commonly think of as incorporeal—may or may not live on after we die. But that we are born and grow and ultimately die as physical, bodily beings is beyond question.

It is also true that, with rare exceptions, our bodies all have certain basic features in common. We have sense organs that enable us to experience the world around us, internal organs that enable us to breathe and digest food and excrete waste, limbs that enable us to move about and manipulate the objects in our environment. And, again with rare exceptions, our bodies are gendered either male or female, which (even apart from pervasive cultural messages about gender) defines who we are in fundamental ways. Our sense of *self*, what makes each of us unique, and our sense of *humanness*, what all of us have in common, are both intrinsically related to our bodily existence.

Finally, our bodily experience, for all its variability, is remarkably universal. We all begin as tiny, helpless infants and grow by stages through puberty, adulthood, and (if we are fortunate) old age. Our bodies make us vulnerable to injury, disease, and pain—who does not remember an early childhood experience of being ill or falling and skinning one's knee? And as we age, our bodies gradually decline in vitality and increase in frailty. But these same bodies also enable us largely to master our world, to develop relationships with others, to climb mountains, to create art, and to build bridges. In short, our bodies are essential to our humanness, our individuality, our sociality, and our identity.

All these facts are commonplace, so much so that it may seem unnecessary to rehearse them here. Yet, precisely because so much of the time we simply take for granted our physicality, we rarely give much thought to the implications of these most basic features of our existence. If we take just a moment to reflect on it, we quickly realize that our bodies are the source of enormous power, but also of enormous vulnerability and powerlessness. And, unlike other creatures that presumably have little or no ability to reflect on these aspects of their physical existence, we have the privilege

107

(and burden) of facing a host of questions—about training, beautifying, cultivating, or abusing our bodies; the proper and improper ends to which they can be used; the ways in which they are perceived by others; the value of pursuing certain experiences of physical pleasure; and, in general, the ways in which we will relate to our bodies. Indeed, these issues are so pervasive that virtually every moral problem we face has a "bodily" component. It is altogether appropriate, then, that this first volume in the series "Jewish Choices, Jewish Voices" concerns questions of responsibilities toward our bodies. (Bodily questions also, of course, include sexual issues; but a separate, full volume in this series will consider those.)

The Heart of the Matter

If we step back from all the issues that arise in relation to the treatment of our bodies, we can identify two fundamental (and closely related) questions at the heart of our subject:

1. What prerogatives do we have with respect to our bodies—that is, what may we do with and to our bodies and what ought we not to do?

2. What ideals do we have for our bodies—that is, how do we imagine the optimal state of our bodies?

The many specific moral questions raised in this volume—by the case studies, the sources, and the short essays that make up our symposium—can be clarified if we frame them in relation to these basic questions.

How we think about a host of specific issues—from dieting to tattooing to engaging in risky behaviors—depends on how we conceptualize our prerogatives with respect to our bodies as well as the ideal state that we wish our bodies to attain. And, it will quickly be noted, the answers to these questions are not determined by anything in the nature of our bodies themselves, but by the *values* that we hold. This will be readily apparent if we reflect for a moment on how we would view the following individuals' treatment of their bodies.

- A student who drinks caffeine in order to stay up late to finish his work for a course; the same student who takes hallucinogenic drugs to experience a high.
- A person who diets to lose weight because she is obese and wants to reduce her risk of heart-related illness; the same person who diets to please her boyfriend; the same person who diets because she is anorexic and feels irrationally compelled to deprive herself of basic nourishment.

- A person who undergoes plastic surgery to repair damage caused by a severe burn; the same person who undergoes surgery to enlarge her breasts because it will improve the likelihood of her being chosen to star in a new film.

In each of these cases, the behavior in question is the same—taking drugs that alter the state of the body, dieting, undergoing plastic surgery—but the motivation and goal are different. We are inclined to treat these situations differently because there are some goals that we believe are valid—academic achievement, prolonging life, and restoring our bodies to their natural state after they have been injured. Other goals we are less sure about insofar as they involve the risk of injury or are pursued for less than noble reasons. It is important, then, as we consider and evaluate the ethics of how we treat our bodies that we bear in mind the *motivations* behind any particular behavior and the *goals* for which it is pursued.

In a sense, there is nothing surprising about this. We always evaluate particular actions within the larger context in which they occur, which typically includes not only questions of motivation but the life history and circumstances of the actors involved and the foreseeable consequences of those actions. So, to consider again the cases just mentioned, we would probably evaluate the ethics of taking hallucinogens differently if the person doing so were part of a clinical study under close supervision of a physician. Similarly, we might well respond differently to the ethics of elective plastic surgery if the woman seeking the film role was a single mother struggling to care for her children with no other readily available means of supporting herself. In short, the life goals that we value—whether they be education or providing for our children, promoting health or contributing to a research study—will play a very significant role in determining how we evaluate what we do with and to our bodies.

One further, and very significant, additional factor needs to be noted here. We often think of our bodies as our exclusive possession, and with good reason. After all, when I stub my toe, *I* am the one who feels the pain. Similarly, we reason, when I take drugs, *I* am the one who will bear the consequences. But there is a flaw in this way of framing questions about our responsibilities to our bodies. For, although my body is very much mine in most respects, what happens to it and how I use it may (and generally does) affect others, sometimes profoundly. This is especially the case if I am in a committed relationship with another adult or if I am responsible for the care of others. But more generally the very fact

109

that we are all social beings, part of a web of relationships that includes family and friends, employers and co-workers, means that what happens to us invariably affects others in our society. In a still more indirect way, the very fact that we are part of the body politic means that what we do to our bodies may trigger responses from government agencies and others who are responsible for the welfare of society as a whole. So, while I may own my house, I am not free to burn it down if doing so endangers the homes of others. Similarly, my body may be my own, but I am not free to do whatever I please with it. If I purposely or recklessly contract an infectious disease, I may threaten the health of others; if I ride my motorcycle without a helmet, I may suffer a concussion and end up in the emergency room of a public hospital being cared for at taxpayer expense. As John Donne put it so eloquently, "No man is an island," and it follows that no one's body is entirely his or her own, no matter how much we may be inclined—or wish—to think otherwise.

The second key issue that shapes the ethics of how we treat our bodies concerns our concept of the ideal body. Of course, no one's body is "perfect," in the sense that every body has its flaws and limitations, even if we consider just the range of normal variation. Some of us are born with specific deformities or impairments. All of us, as we now know from genetics, are born with genes that determine our proclivities to develop certain diseases or respond adversely to certain drugs or lack some physical ability that others may have. But all the same, biology is not necessarily destiny. We can perform surgery to correct abnormalities, take medicine to correct for chemical imbalances in our bodies, and train our bodies to do things that do not come easily. What ethical considerations arise when we attempt to make our bodies "better," closer to some "ideal" of functioning that we have adopted?

This question is complicated by the fact that we tend to define what is acceptable in terms of what is "natural" or "optimal" in relation to certain basic functions. Almost no one would argue that we should simply accept our bodies in their natural state, refusing to do anything at all to improve upon their natural abilities. The primary goal of medicine, after all, is precisely to heal—to remove those impediments that prevent us from functioning as well as we could. But there is a wide spectrum of possibilities here, and most of us would differentiate between taking an antibiotic to fight an infection or undergoing bypass surgery to improve the functioning of our heart and taking performance-enhancing drugs to compete more effectively in athletics. And yet, the acceptability of any of these medical interventions depends on how we understand the ideal state that we are trying to create (or restore) in our bodies.

To some extent, of course, this ideal state is a cultural construct. Americans will very likely view this differently from Italians or Indonesians, and Americans in the twenty-first century certainly tend to endorse a different ideal from what they did in the eighteenth century. Moreover, what is ideal for one individual may be utterly unacceptable for another. If I were a model or a performing artist or a professional athlete, I might well have different physical needs, different thresholds of pain, different ideas of the kinds of medical interventions needed to support my chosen profession from those I have as a college professor. As long as they are functioning in a basically healthy way, our bodies are as close to ideal as they need to be. Those whose livelihood depends on the use of particular, highly developed physical traits will likely have different ideals from mine. The same could be said of those whose cultural status depends, for example, on bearing children or achieving a certain physical stature.

Finally, precisely because people with different physical abilities and cultural expectations hold different ideals of the body, they will also assess differently the benefits and risks involved in any particular use of the body (or medical treatment thereof). The life stage of the individual involved will also be a factor here. We can reasonably expect that a single man in his twenties and a married man in his sixties would have rather different senses of what it means to have an ideal body and so too how much risk one is willing to take—either in the pursuit of physical pleasure or in the service of correcting a physical impairment.

This last point highlights the fact that our perspective on our bodies, and so our sense of moral responsibility toward them, varies widely from one culture to another. Jewish culture has its own unique set of values about the goals and purposes of the body as well as distinctive images of the ideal body, which give rise to a whole set of moral guidelines. Because a number of the other pieces in this volume discuss these in some detail, we will comment here only briefly on this aspect of our subject.

Jewish Bodies

Much has been made of the Jewish view that our bodies belong ultimately to God, not to us. It follows, as many have said, that we may not injure or endanger ourselves, even if in our own view the benefits of doing so outweigh the risks. This is all true, yet it is with respect to the ultimate *purpose,* rather than the ultimate *source,* of our bodies that Judaism offers its most profound and far-reaching guidance. The supreme goal of human life, and especially of Jewish life, is to know and serve God. We do this primarily, according to Jewish tradition, through observing God's commandments as these have been laid out in the Torah and in the vast rabbinic commentary to it. It follows that our bodies are designed to facilitate our relationship with God in all its aspects. This perspective has important implications for many of the ethical issues raised in this volume.

First, it suggests that the body is not an end in itself but a means to a religious end. The body is a vessel for the soul and is valued primarily for this reason. Jewish tradition is replete with admonitions to study, to pray, and to serve God wholeheartedly; and, of course, without a healthy body all of these become far more difficult. But it is hard to find exhortations within the tradition to cultivate and preserve the body in order to make it more beautiful, powerful, or effective in mastering the arts of civilization. This is hardly surprising in a religious tradition that regarded the body as transitory, while the soul was pure and immortal.

From this perspective, treatment of the body is likewise a means to an end. It is essential that we take good care of the body, for only in this way can we properly serve God. If we are unable to hear, speak, or walk, we will be unable to do some of those things that God expects of us; these impairments should, therefore, properly be rectified to the extent possible. If, on the other hand, we are not beautiful enough or do not have sufficient stamina to run a marathon, the tradition would be far less certain about the value of corrective medical interventions. So the way in which we think about the proper purpose and value of our bodies will decisively shape how we define our prerogatives and, therefore, the parameters of our moral responsibilities toward them.

But, of course, Judaism also teaches us to praise God for the wondrous workings of the body, for these are truly expressions of God's creative power. The message here is powerful and far reaching. The intricate workings of the human body are a wonder and not infrequently a source of amazement even for physicians who think of themselves as largely secular.[1] It is important that this sense of awe is not restricted to bodies

---

1. See Louis E. Newman, "Ethics, Faith and Healing: Jewish Physicians Reflect on Medical Practice," in *Caring Well: Religion, Narrative and Health Care Ethics,* edited by David H. Smith (Louisville, KY: Westminster John Knox Press, 2000), 117–43.

that conform to a particular cultural ideal. Indeed, the rabbis require that we recite a blessing upon seeing a person with a physical disability: "Blessed are You, Lord our God, who fashions diverse creatures." Seeing a body that is "abnormal" is no less cause for praising God than seeing one that looks like a Greek statue. This teaching entails a striking reversal of many commonly held American values. The fact that we have bodies at all—and the further fact that our bodies come in such diverse forms and conditions—is far more significant than endorsing any particular ideal type of body.

All of this does not militate against the view of the classical Jewish tradition that there are certain things we should and should not do to our bodies. Boys' bodies are to be circumcised on the eighth day; women are to purify their bodies each month following their menstrual period. Bodies are not to be mutilated or defaced through tattooing; even the bodies of the dead are not to be altered unnecessarily through autopsy or embalming. These requirements and restrictions on the treatment of the body are undoubtedly over-determined—that is, rooted in more than one value. What is clear is that Jewish teaching has viewed the body as a testament to God's creative power, a vehicle for serving God, and a container for the divinely imparted soul.

Needless to say, Jewish tradition encompasses more than just these religious values, important as they are. The biblical stories of fertility and barrenness, so often associated with blessings and curses, respectively, contain many implicit messages about the value and purpose of our bodies. Similarly, the biblical and rabbinic portrayal of relationships between men and women have deeply impressed themselves into the Jewish psyche, so much so that many otherwise very liberal Jews today still find it difficult to accept women as rabbis because religious authority is associated exclusively with men. These cultural images continue to exert a powerful influence over many contemporary Jews, whether or not they feel deeply connected to Jewish religious rituals and values surrounding the treatment of the body.

Wrestling with the Jewish Tradition and Contemporary Culture

In all, Jewish tradition has bequeathed to us a rich legacy of religious values and cultural images, some of which seem profound and spiritually uplifting, others of which may feel outmoded or stifling, still others of which may need to be reinterpreted and reappropriated in order to play a meaningful role in our lives. To further complicate matters, most contemporary Jews, especially in North America, live at the crossroads of secular, Western culture and Jewish culture. To leave either of these cultures entirely behind would feel at the very least uncomfortable; for some, it would be utterly inconceivable. Finding a way to accommodate both sets of values, forging a synthesis, however unstable, between them, is precisely the challenge that contemporary Western Jews face. The authors who have contributed essays to this volume, like the readers for whom this series is intended, live in this tension, sometimes embracing the struggle that this entails, sometimes resisting it.

Against the background of what we said earlier about the general and specifically Jewish issues that arise in connection with treatment of the body, we can readily identify some of these tensions in balancing tradition with modernity among the contributors to our symposium. Abraham Twerski presents and unapologetically endorses fundamental Jewish values found within the tradition. Harry Brod struggles with and ultimately seems inclined to reject the ritual of male circumcision, insofar as it perpetuates a tradition of patriarchy that he finds at odds with contemporary values. Samuel Kunin, in contrast, calls on his long career as a urologist to urge the importance of circumcision for medical as well as religious reasons. Andy Abrams and Rebecca Alpert write about the potential value of tattooing, despite the clear and persistent prohibition against it within traditional Jewish sources. Both appreciate the potentially positive expressions of Jewish identity that can result when Jewish words and images are inscribed on one's body. Adam Goodkind offers a positive assessment of some traditional Jewish values concerning the body insofar as they seem pragmatic and commonsensical, even if he can no longer subscribe to the religious beliefs that gave rise to those values. Miriyam Glazer and Lori Lefkovitz seek to sort through the very complicated and conflicting messages that Jewish tradition and culture have sent Jewish women over the ages. Their goal is to find a way to reappropriate and accentuate some of the positive components of the tradition, those that nurture healthy relationships between women and their bodies.

Judith Rabinor, who has had extensive clinical experience dealing with the devastating effects of eating disorders, attempts to account for the ways in which Judaism both contributes to distorted images of the body and provides important resources for healing. Lenny Krayzelburg, though not deeply rooted in Jewish tradition while growing up in Russia, feels that his own career as an Olympic champion has taught him much about how to think about the body, messages that he finds echoed in some Jewish values. Finally, Judith Levitan and Robert Karasov reflect on the problem of resolving the inner tension they feel when their own Jewish values conflict with the desires and values of their patients.

These essays, taken together, testify forcefully that contemporary Jews from all walks of life and backgrounds are engaged in a serious quest to understand the import for their lives of Judaism's teachings about the body. These efforts are profoundly personal; and, at the same time, they are part of a common communal attempt among Jews to reclaim those teachings that speak to the very contemporary dilemmas we face. Sometimes contemporary Jews express surprise that those ancient sources remain an abiding source of wisdom; sometimes they distance themselves from traditional views and restrictions that no longer make sense or even feel oppressive. But whatever their stance in relation to these traditional perspectives, modern Jews are fully engaged in dialogue with them; open to learning what they have to offer; and willing to adopt, adapt or reject. The only thing they refuse to do is to ignore the tradition entirely. In this sense, they provide wonderful models for all contemporary Jews who take seriously the possibility that Judaism in all its complexity remains a vivid and vital voice in their lives.

What Lies Ahead

We have focused in this volume on just a few moral issues related to the treatment of the body in the hope that these would prove illustrative, provocative, and particularly relevant to contemporary readers. It would be well beyond the scope of this volume, and probably of any single volume, to provide a comprehensive survey of all the issues that our embodiment raises. In closing, though, it might be valuable to sketch just a few of the many other sorts of issues on the horizon that involve our bodies, for this will enable us to see how daunting the problems we face are.

The extraordinary advances in medical technology in recent decades have already transformed the treatment of the body. The diagnosis and treatment of cancer, heart disease, and HIV/AIDS are vastly better than they were just a decade ago. It is sometimes difficult to remember that within the lifetimes of your editors organ transplantation and assisted

115

reproduction have changed from being wildly experimental to being routine. What we once only dreamed of we now take for granted. Much of this can be attributed to the development of new drugs, treatment procedures, and technologies such as CT scanning. Throughout developed countries, improvements in public health—especially health education—and safety have significantly lengthened life expectancy, to say nothing of quality of life.

But it is the decoding of the human genome that promises to truly revolutionize the way we treat our bodies. As we come to know more and more about the ways in which our bodies are programmed at the most basic cellular level, we will be able to detect the presence of illness like high blood pressure many years before symptoms of the disease occur. We will also understand which groups of drugs will be most effective for which patients, taking much of the guesswork out of treatment options and drastically improving results. Stem cell research is just beginning to point toward as yet undreamed of possibilities for regenerating damaged tissues and organs.

If all this were not enough, we are just on the verge of major breakthroughs in our understanding of the brain, which promise to revolutionize our ability to treat a great many neurological and psychological impairments. Some have begun experimenting with the implantation of electronic devices in our bodies to treat diseases such as Parkinson's. Before long, other complex, humanly-made devices will almost certainly be developed to augment or replace failing body parts in ways that will make prosthetic limbs and pacemakers seem archaic by comparison. The boundary between the body as a natural phenomenon and the body as a constructed, mechanized, or even automated commodity may very well become blurred.

These technological developments place within our hands vast new powers to heal and transform the human body in ways that are at least as far reaching as the development of vaccines and antibiotics in the twentieth century. How will we handle these new abilities? How will we resist the temptation, already evident in debates over organ donation and commercial surrogacy, to commodify our bodies—that is, to treat them as commodities that can be bought and sold? These issues are further complicated by the fact that these new powers are emerging just as the baby-boomer generation, already accustomed to a higher level of medical care than any previous generation in history, is aging and requiring more medical care. As genetic engineering moves from science fiction to clinical reality, how will we prevent people (especially those with adequate financial resources) from designing children to their specifications? Even more basic, how will we respond to the fifty-year-old woman who wants to bear children—even now some women are doing that—or the seventy-year-old man who wants the drugs that will make his body work as if he were less than half that age? Each possibility of manipulating, repairing, treating, or improving our bodies raises new versions of age-old questions: What may we do with our bodies? What ends are appropriate, and what means are appropriate for achieving those ends? What sort of body is ideal, and how vigorously do we wish to pursue that ideal? Does there come a time when we should accept diminishing bodily abilities and even death? If so, how do we know when that time has come? (We will deal with some of these questions in a future volume in this series on medical ethics.)

A brave new world is dawning, one for which we are scarcely prepared. Even the experts in these fields cannot tell us with any certainty how these new abilities will alter our relationships to our bodies. The fact that we will continue to rely on our bodies is certain, as is the fact that there will continue to be very strong pressures exerted—by scientific researchers, corporate interests, and the media—to extend our control over our bodies to the greatest degree possible. The vulnerability to which we referred at the outset of this essay may be gradually, or even rapidly, minimized as the scope and sophistication of our control over bodily processes increases exponentially. But it is not at all clear whether this is an unmitigated good or whether it will simply bring in its wake a whole new set of challenges to our collective well-being.

What role can Judaism usefully play in addressing such unprecedented and complex problems? Where will our children and their children, for whom these developments will seem as commonplace as a blood test is for us, look to find moral guidance?

Concluding Personal Reflections

We cannot know the answers to these questions, nor do we think it prudent to speculate. What seems clear to us, though, is that at least some of the concepts and values found within Jewish tradition will prove useful as we confront these issues. Without attempting to indicate precisely what sorts of guidance will emerge, let us point to at least a few of these values.

We believe it will continue to be important to acknowledge, first and foremost, that our bodies are awesome in their complexity. Whether we take our bodies to be the work of a divine Creator or not, our growing knowledge of the *mechanics* of the body will need to be balanced by a sustained reverence for the *mystery* of the body.

We also believe that our ever-growing ability to control and manipulate our bodies to serve our own ends will increasingly encourage us to glorify our own power and mastery over nature. This godlike power, already evident in the medical care available today, must be tempered by humility and restraint, lest we forget that power is not synonymous with wisdom and that mastery does not confer maturity.

We believe that Jews, insofar as they continue to wish to preserve a distinctive religious-cultural identity, will need to express that identity in and through their bodies. The particular rituals prescribed and the specific behaviors proscribed may change—rituals invariably evolve within religious traditions in response to changing needs and circumstances. But there is no more powerful or visible or enduring way to create and sustain identity than through bodily experience.

Finally, we believe that as the general culture continues to emphasize certain goals—bodily pleasure, autonomy, beautification, sexual gratification, and the control of all bodily functions—Jews (and many others) will continue to seek other ways of framing the treatment of the body. These ways may not rely centrally on belief in God or religious imperatives, but they will consider treatment of the body in relation to other, transcendent goals and in light of values that place the body in service of nonbodily, or spiritual, concerns. Evidence of this trend is widespread among many religious groups today who, like Jews, do not at all reject the benefits of modern medical advances in the care of the body but just as surely do not adopt uncritically all the American values about the body that typically accompany them.

That Judaism does, and will continue to, offer resources to counterbalance these cultural trends is plain enough. What remains to be seen is just how and to what extent Jews will avail themselves of them. If the evidence of this volume is any indication, we have reason to be hopeful.

E.N.D.

L.E.N.

Glossary

adamah Ground.

brit milah Circumcision. Traditionally performed on a baby boy on the eighth day following his birth. See Genesis 17.

chai life.

challah/challot The special twisted egg bread traditionally made for the Sabbath and other Jewish holidays.

dina d'malkhuta dina "The law of the land is the law." The talmudic rule that Jews are subject to the legal authority of the non-Jewish societies in which they live (B. Nedarim 28a; Gittin 10b; Bava Kamma 113a; Bava Batra 54b–55a).

dover emet bilvavo lit., "speaking honestly in one's heart." Being honest with oneself.

Ehyeh asher ehyeh "I Am-Was-Will Be Who/What I Am-Was-Will Be." The explanation God offers to Moses of God's name, meant to emphasize the impenetrable mystery of God's nature or perhaps God's transcending of time or causality. See Exodus 3:14.

goy/goyim Lit., "nation(s), non-Jew(s)." Sometimes used with derogatory connotations.

halakhah Jewish law.

Havdalah Lit. "separation." The ceremony that separates the Sabbath from the rest of the week.

hesed Lit., "lovingkindness." One of the qualities of God and one of the virtues that Jews aspire to emulate.

hevruta Lit., "partner." In traditional Jewish text study, students work in pairs.

hiddur mitzvah Lit., "beautification of a commandment." Traditional concept that a biblical commandment should be performed in a way that is aesthetically pleasing and uplifting, rather than perfunctory.

kashrut "Kosher." The dietary rules prescribed by the Torah and observed by traditional Jews. See Leviticus 11 and Deuteronomy 14.

kavanah "Intention." A concept with wide-ranging application in Jewish law, especially in relation to the proper performance of a ritual act or in matters of liability in civil and criminal affairs.

kavod Honor. Frequently used in connection with the honor due one's parents or, more generally, of honoring God's creatures.

kiddush Lit., "sanctification." The prayer said over a cup of wine at the beginning of Sabbath and holiday meals.

klei kodesh Holy instruments (or holy articles). Sometimes used metaphorically for rabbis, cantors, and Jewish educators.

koach Force, power.

kol Yisrael arevim ze le ze "All Jews are responsible for one another" (B. Shevu'ot 39a) This Talmudic phrase reflects the strong traditional values of Jews' interdependence and their collective responsibility.

kup Lit., "head" (Yiddish). Used figuratively as well as literally, as in "He has a good *kup* for Talmud study."

lifnim meshurat hadin Supererogation; doing more than the law requires (or pressing one's legal claims less than the law permits).

lo tishkach "Never forget."

malach/malachim "Messenger(s)" (whether human or divine).

mechitzah A partition separating men and women in Orthodox synagogues.

mensch/menschlichkeit Lit. "man/humanity" (Yiddish). Refers to the popular traditional concept of human decency; one who is morally honorable and sensitive to the needs of others is said to be a mensch.

middat ha-din The attribute of strict justice. One of God's two main attributes in relationship with humankind; see next entry.

middat ha-rachamim The attribute of mercy or compassion. God's other, countervailing, attribute.

mikveh Ritual bath. Used by women for purification after the conclusion of their menstrual periods before reestablishing sexual relations with their husbands, also as part of the ritual for conversation to Judaism and in other instances of ritual or spiritual purification. See Leviticus 15 and Numbers 19.

minyan Lit., "quorum." The ten adults (traditionally, ten adult men) required to constitute a quorum for purposes of public prayer.

Mi Shebairach A prayer for healing named for the first two words of the traditional Hebrew text, "May the one who blessed . . . [our ancestors . . . bless those who are ill . . .]."

mishkan Lit., "dwelling place." The name of the ancient Tabernacle that the Israelites carried with them during their wanderings in the desert. The Tabernacle, and later the permanent Temple in Jerusalem, were understood as the place where God's presence dwelled on earth.

Mishnah Lit. "teaching." The name of the Hebrew law code written in Palestine in circa 200 C.E., traditionally ascribed to Rabbi Judah the Prince. The Mishnah greatly expands on biblical law and later becomes the foundation of the Talmud.

mitzvah/mitzvot "Commandment(s)." One of the Torah's laws. According to tradition, there were 613 divinely ordained mitzvot in the Torah.

mohel Ritual circumcisor.

niggun Lit, "melody." One of the haunting wordless melodies sung by Hasidic Jews.

ona'ah Lit. "coercion." Unfair exploitation through overcharging.

parashah Torah portion. The set reading from the Pentateuch for a given Sabbath or holiday, usually encompassing several chapters.

Rosh Hodesh The new moon, which marks the beginning of the new month on the Hebrew calendar. Some contemporary Jewish women have created ceremonies to celebrate Rosh Hodesh.

ruach Spirit.

selichot Petitions for forgiveness.

shtetl One of the small, predominantly Jewish villages of eastern Europe from which many Jews emigrated to America or Israel.

shtetl *bubbes* Jewish grandmothers.

Shulchan Aruch "The set table." The name of the classic code of Jewish law composed by Rabbi Joseph Caro (1488–1575) and completed in 1565.

teshuvah "An answer." A rabbinic ruling in response to a question in Jewish law. Also, lit., "turning" or "response"; repentance, one of the key moral aspects of Jewish life.

tikkun olam Lit., "repair of the world." The idea, central to Jewish tradition, that it is the task of humankind to complete the process of creation that God began. The concept takes on special cosmological significance in the work of the Kabbalists, or Jewish mystics.

tikvah Hope.

tokhehah "Obligation to reprove [those who transgress]." See Leviticus 19:17.

tzeniut Lit., "modesty." Used most often in connection with the traditional value that women should dress in a way that is not revealing or sexually provocative.

yetzer ha-ra Lit., "evil inclination." That aspect of human nature that prompts us to sin.

zachor Remember.

Suggestions for Further Reading

General Sources on Jewish Ethics

Abramowitz, Yosef I., and Susan Silverman. *Jewish Family & Life: Traditions, Holidays, and Values for Today's Parents and Children.* New York: Golden Books, 1997.

Agus, Jacob B. *The Vision and the Way: An Interpretation of Jewish Ethics.* New York: Frederick Ungar Publishing Co., 1966.

Alpert, Rebecca T., and Jacob J. Staub. *Exploring Judaism: A Reconstructionist Approach.* Expanded and Updated. Jenkintown, Pa.: Jewish Reconstructionist Federation, 2000.

Amsel, Nachum. *The Jewish Encyclopedia of Moral and Ethical Issues.* Northvale, N.J.: Jason Aronson, 1994.

Birnbaum, Philip. *Encyclopedia of Jewish Concepts.* New York: Hebrew Publishing Company, 1964, 1995.

Borowitz, Eugene B. *Exploring Jewish Ethics: Papers on Covenant Responsibility.* Detroit, Mich.: Wayne State University Press, 1990.

_____, ed. *Reform Jewish Ethics and the Halakhah.* West Orange, N.J.: Behrman House, 1994.

_____ and Frances Weinman Schwartz. *The Jewish Moral Virtues.* Philadelphia: The Jewish Publication Society, 1999.

Breslauer, S. Daniel. *A New Jewish Ethics.* New York & Toronto: Edwin Mellon Press, 1983.

Cohen, Jeffery. *Dear Chief Rabbi: From the Correspondence of Chief Rabbi Immanuel Jakobovits on Matters of Jewish Law, Ethics, and Contemporary Issues, 1980–1990.* Hoboken, N.J.: Ktav, 1995.

Cohn, Haim. *Human Rights in Jewish Law.* New York: Ktav Publishing [Institute of Jewish Affairs, London], 1984.

Dan, Joseph. *Jewish Mysticism and Jewish Ethics.* Philadelphia: The Jewish Publication Society and University of Washington Press, 1986.

Dorff, Elliot N. "The Ethics of Judaism." In *The Blackwell Companion to Judaism.* Ed. Jacob Neusner and Alan J. Avery-Peck, 373–392. Oxford: Blackwell Publishers, 2000.

_____. *Love Your Neighbor and Yourself: A Jewish Approach to Modern Personal Ethics.* Philadelphia: The Jewish Publication Society, 2003.

_____. *Matters of Life and Death: A Jewish Approach to Modern Medical Ethics.* Philadelphia: The Jewish Publication Society, 1998.

_____. *To Do the Right and the Good: A Jewish Approach to Modern Personal Ethics.* Philadelphia: The Jewish Publication Society, 2002.

_____. *The Way into Tikkun Olam (Fixing the World).* Woodstock, Vt.: Jewish Lights, 2005.

_____ and Louis E. Newman, eds. *Contemporary Jewish Ethics and Morality: A Reader.* New York: Oxford University Press, 1995.

_____ and Arthur Rosett. *A Living Tree: The Roots and Growth of Jewish Law.* Albany: State University of New York Press, 1988.

Dresner, Samuel H., and Byron L. Sherwin. *Judaism: The Way of Sanctification.* New York: United Synagogue of America, 1978.

Fox, Marvin, ed. *Modern Jewish Ethics: Theory and Practice.* Columbus: Ohio State University Press, 1975.

Freund, Richard A. *Understanding Jewish Ethics.* 2 vols. Lewiston, N.Y.: Edwin Mellon Press, 1990 (vol. 1), 1993 (vol.2).

Goldman, Alex J. *Judaism Confronts Contemporary Issues.* New York: Shengold Publishers, 1978.

Goldstein, Niles E., and Steven S. Mason. *Judaism and Spiritual Ethics.* New York: Union of American Hebrew Congregations Press, 1996.

Goodman, Lenn E. *Judaism, Human Rights, and Human Values.* New York: Oxford University Press, 1998.

Gordis, Robert. *The Dynamics of Judaism: A Study in Jewish Law.* Bloomington: Indiana University Press, 1990.

_____. *Judaic Ethics for a Lawless World.* New York: Jewish Theological Seminary of America, 1986.

Jacobs, Louis. *Jewish Personal and Social Ethics.* West Orange, N.J.: Behrman House, 1990.

Kadushin, Max. *Worship and Ethics: A Study in Rabbinic Judaism.* Evanston, Ill.: Northwestern University Press, 1964.

Kaplan, Mordecai M. *The Future of the American Jew.* New York: Reconstructionist Press, 1948, 1967. (See especially chapter 15 on Jewish ethics.)

Kellner, Menachem Marc, ed. *Contemporary Jewish Ethics.* New York: Sanhedrin Press, 1978.

Klagsbrun, Francine. *Voices of Wisdom: Jewish Ideas and Ethics for Everyday Living.* New York: Pantheon Books, 1980.

123

Malsin, Simeon J., ed. *Gates of Mitzvah—Shaarei Mitzvah*. New York: Central Conference of American Rabbis Press, 1986.

Meir, Asher. *The Jewish Ethicist: Everyday Ethics for Business and Life.* Jersey City, N.J.: Ktav and Business Ethics Center of Jerusalem, 2005.

Newman, Louis E. *An Introduction to Jewish Ethics.* Upper Saddle River, N.J.: Pearson Prentice Hall, 2005.

_____. *Past Imperatives: Studies in the History and Theory of Jewish Ethics.* Albany: State University of New York Press, 1998.

Novak, David. *Jewish Social Ethics.* New York : Oxford University Press, 1992.

Olitzky, Kerry M., and Rachel T. Sabath. *Striving Toward Virtue: A Contemporary Guide for Jewish Ethical Behavior.* Hoboken, N.J.: Ktav, 1996.

Sacks, Jonathan. *To Heal a Fractured World: The Ethics of Responsibility.* New York: Schocken Books, 2005.

Schwarz, Sidney. *Judaism and Justice: The Jewish Passion to Repair the World.* Woodstock, Vt,: Jewish Lights, 2006.

Shatz, David, Chaim I. Waxman, and Nathan J. Diament, eds. *Tikkun Olam: Social Responsibility in Jewish Thought and Law.* Northvale, N.J.: Jason Aronson, 1997.

Sherwin, Byron L. *Jewish Ethics for the Twenty-First Century: Living in the Image of God.* Syracuse, N.Y.: Syracuse University Press, 2000.

Sherwin, Byron L. and Seymour J. Cohen. *Creating An Ethical Jewish Life: A Practical Introduction to Classic Teachings on How to Be a Jew.* Woodstock, Vt.: Jewish Lights, 2001.

_____. *How to Be a Jew: Ethical Teachings of Judaism.* Northvale, N.J.: Jason Aronson, 1992.

Siegel, Richard, Michael Strassfield, and Sharon Strassfield, eds. *The Jewish Catalogue.* Philadelphia: The Jewish Publication Society of America, 1973.

Stone, Ira. *A Responsible Life: The Spiritual Path of Mussar.* New York: Aviv Press of the Rabbinical Assembly, 2006.

Telushkin, Joseph. *Jewish Wisdom: Ethical, Spiritual, and Historical Lessons from the Great Works and Thinkers.* New York: William Morrow & Co., 1994.

_____. *A Code of Jewish Ethics.* Vol. 1: *You Shall Be Holy.* New York: Bell Tower, 2006.

Vorspan, Albert, and David Saperstein. *Tough Choices: Jewish Perspectives on Social Justice.* New York: Union of American Hebrew Congregations Press, 1992.

Washofsky, Mark. *Jewish Living: A Guide to Contemporary Reform Practice.* New York: Union of American Hebrew Congregations, 2001.

Wurzburger, Walter S. *Ethics of Responsibility: Pluralistic Approaches to Covenantal Ethics.* Philadelphia: The Jewish Publication Society, 1994.

Jewish Sources on the Ethical Issues Concerning the Body

Aberbach, Moses. "Smoking and the Halakhah." *Tradition* 10 (1969): 49–60.

Abraham, Abraham S. *Medical Halacha for Everyone.* New York: Feldheim, 1980.

Bleich, J. David. *Bioethical Dilemmas: A Jewish Perspective.* Hoboken, N.J.: Ktav Publishing House, 1998.

_____. *Judaism and Healing: Halakhic Perspectives.* New York: Ktav Publishing House, 1981.

_____. "Smoking." *Tradition* 16 (1977): 121–123. Reprinted in Elliot N. Dorff and Arthur I. Rosett. *A Living Tree.* Albany: State University of New York Press, 1988.

Brayer, Menachem M. "Drugs: A Jewish View." *Tradition* 10 (1968): 31–41.

Cohen, Jeffery, ed. *Dear Chief Rabbi: From the Correspondence of Chief Rabbi Immanuel Jakobovits on Matters of Jewish Law, Ethics, and Contemporary Issues, 1980–1990.* Hoboken, N.J.: Ktav, 1995.

Dichowsky, Shlomo. "Rescue and Treatment: Halakhic Scales of Priority." *Dine Israel* (1976): 45–66.

Diskind, Meyer, H. "The Jewish Drug Addict: A Challenge to the Jewish Community." In *The Jewish Family in a Changing World.* Ed. Gilbert S. Rosenthal, 122–135. New York: Thomas Yoseloff, 1970.

Dorff, Elliot N. *Matters of Life and Death: A Jewish Approach to Modern Medical Ethics.* Philadelphia: The Jewish Publication Society, 1998.

_____ and Aaron Mackler. "Responsibilities for the Provision of Health Care." In *Life and Death Responsibilities in Jewish Biomedical Ethics.* Ed. Aaron Meckler, chap. 30. New York: Jewish Theological Seminary, 2000. Also in *Responsa, 1991–2000, of the Committee on Jewish Law and Standards of the Conservative Movement.* Ed. Kassel Abelson and David J. Fine, 313–336. New York: Rabbinical Assembly, 2002. Also available at www.rabbinicalassembly.org/law/contemporary_halakhah.html.

Eilberg-Schwartz, Howard, ed. *People of the Body: Jews and Judaism from an Embodied Perspective.* Albany: State University of New York Press, 1992.

Suggestions for Further Reading

Einstein, Stanley. "The Use and Misuse of Alcohol and Other Drugs." In *The Jewish Family in a Changing World.* Ed. Gilbert S. Rosenthal, 81–121. New York: Thomas Yoseloff, 1970.

Feldman, David M. *Health and Medicine in the Jewish Tradition: L'hayyim—To Life.* New York: Crossroad, 1986.

Flancbaum, Louis. ". . . *And You Shall Live By Them": Contemporary Jewish Approaches to Medical Ethics.* Pittsburgh: Mirkov Publications, 2001.

Freedman, Benjamin. *Duty and Healing: Foundations of a Jewish Bioethic.* New York: Routledge, 1999.

Freehof, Solomon B. "Cosmetic Surgery." In *Reform Responsa for Our Time,* inquiry 8. Cincinnati, Ohio: Hebrew Union College Press, 1971.

_____. "Psychodelic Drugs." In *Current Reform Responsa,* chap. 60. Cincinnati, Ohio: Hebrew Union College Press, 1969.

Freeman, David L., and Judith Z. Abrams. *Illness and Health in the Jewish Tradition: Writings from the Bible to Today.* Philadelphia: The Jewish Publication Society, 1999.

Goldson, Yonason. "Son, Skydiving Is Dangerous." Available at www.aish.com/family/mensch/Son3_Skydiving_is_Dangerous.asp (accessed December 6, 2006).

Gurock, Jeffrey S. *Judaism's Encounter with American Sports.* Bloomington: Indiana University Press, 2005.

Hebshi, Shoshana. "Tattoo Jews." *The Jewish News Weekly,* January 16, 2004.

Herring, Basil F. "Smoking and Drugs." In *Jewish Ethics and Halakhah for Our Time: Sources and Commentary,* chap. 9. New York: Ktav Publishing House, 1984.

Lamm, Maurice. "Modesty (Tz'ni'ut)." In *The Jewish Way in Love and Marriage.* New York: Harper & Row, 1980.

Lucas, Alan. "Tattooing and Body Piercing in Jewish Law." In *Responsa 1991–2000: The Committee on Jewish Law and Standards of the Conservative Movement.* Ed. Kassel Abelson and David J. Fine, 115–120. New York: Rabbinical Assembly, 2002. Also available at www.rabbinicalassembly.org/law/contemporary_halakhah.html.

Meier, Levi, ed. *Jewish Values in Bioethics.* New York: Human Sciences Press, 1986.

Novak, David. "Alcohol and Drug Abuse in the Perspective of Jewish Tradition." *Judaism* 33 (1984): 221–232.

Rigler, Sara Yoheved, "Ritalin and Judaism." Available at www.aish.com/family/mensch/Ritalin_and_Judaism.asp (accessed December 10, 2006).

Rosner, Fred. *Biomedical Ethics and Jewish Law.* Hoboken, N.J.: Ktav Publishing House, 2001.

_____. *Modern Medicine and Jewish Ethics.* 2nd rev and augmented ed. Hoboken, N.J.: Ktav and Yeshivah University Press, 1991.

Rosner, Fred, and J. David Bleich, eds. *Jewish Bioethics.* New York: Sanhedrin Press, 1979.

Samson, David. "Something for Everyone: Body Piercing in Jewish Law." *Israel National News,* August 7, 2002. Also available at www.israelnationalnews.com/english/newspaper/torah/ask-rabbi-7-Aug-02.htm (accessed December 6, 2006).

_____. "Tattoos Are Not for Jews." *Israel National News,* July 24, 2002. Also available at www.israelnationalnews.com/english/newspaper/torah/ask-rabbi-24-Jul-02.htm (accessed December 6, 2006).

Shulman, Nisson E., *Jewish Answers to Medical Ethics Questions: Questions and Answers from the Medical Ethics Department of the Office of the Chief Rabbi of Great Britain.* Northvale, N.J.: Jason Aronson, 1998.

Siegel, Danny. *Healing: Readings and Meditations.* Pittsboro, N.C.: Town House Press, 1999.

Siegel, Seymour. "Smoking—A Jewish Perspective." In *Smoking: Is It a Sin?* Tom McDevitt, 50–55. Pocatello: Little Red Hen, Inc. 1980. Reprinted in *A Living Tree: the Roots and Growth of Jewish Law.* Eds. Elliot N. Dorff and Arthur I. Rossett, 355–359. Albany: State University of New York Press, 1988. Also reprinted in *Life and Death Responsibilities in Jewish Biomedical Ethics.* Ed. Aaron L. Mackler, chap. 32. Jewish Theological Seminary of America, 2000.

_____. "Suicide in the Jewish View." *Conservative Judaism* 32 (1978): 67–74.

Steinberg, Avraham. *Encyclopedia of Jewish Medical Ethics.* 3 vols. Trans. by Fred Rosner. Jerusalem and New York: Feldheim Publishers, 2003.

Steinmetz, Chaim. "Is Smoking Kosher?" *Jewish Law Commentary.* Available at www.jlaw.com/Commentary/smoking.html.

Strassfield, Michael. "Awakening to the Day." In *A Book of Life: Embracing Judaism as a Spiritual Practice.* New York: Schocken Books, 2002.

Teutsch, David A. *Bioethics: Reinvigorating the Practice of Contemporary Jewish Ethics.* Wyncote, Pa.: Reconstructionist Rabbinical College Press, 2005.

Suggestions for Further Reading

Tirosh-Samuelson, Hava, ed. *Women and Gender in Jewish Philosophy.* Bloomington: Indiana University Press, 2004.

Washofsky, Mark. "Medical Ethics." In *Jewish Living: A Guide to Contemporary Reform Practice.* New York: Union of American Hebrew Congregations Press, 2001. Also available at www.myjewishlearning.com/daily_life/TheBody/Health_Healing/smoking_alcohol_drugs.htm.

Yarden, Orphen. "Anti-Semitic Perceptions of the Jewish Body." Available at www.myjewishlearning.com/daily_life/TheBody/Body_Th_and_Th/Antisemitic_Stereotypes.htm (accessed December 6, 2006).

Editors and Contributors

Editors

Elliot N. Dorff is rector and the Sol and Anne Dorff Distinguished Professor of Philosophy at the American Jewish University (formerly the University of Judaism) in Los Angeles. He is an ordained rabbi and the author of 12 books, including three award-winning Jewish Publication Society books on Jewish ethics, and has edited several anthologies, including two with Louis Newman: *Contemporary Jewish Ethics and Morality* (1995) and *Contemporary Jewish Theology* (1999). Since 1984 he has served on the Rabbinical Assembly's Committee of Jewish Law and Standards, currently as its chair. He has also served on three federal government commissions dealing with health care, sexual ethics, and protections of humans in research, and he currently serves on the California Ethics Committee governing embryonic stem cell research.

Louis E. Newman is the John M. and Elizabeth W. Musser Professor of Religious Studies and director of Judaic Studies at Carleton College. He is the author of *Past Imperatives: Studies in the History and Theory of Jewish Ethics* (1998) and *An Introduction to Jewish Ethics* (2005) as well as co-editor with Elliot Dorff of two anthologies (see above). He is currently working on a book on Jewish views of repentance.

Contributors

Andy Abrams has lived in Los Angeles and worked in film and television for the last four years, including time with Francis Ford Coppola's American Zoetrope. He has a degree in anthropology from Antioch College. He is deeply interested in examining the balance between individuality and a sense of belonging, as well as the complexities of Jewish identity. He was raised in an observant Jewish household, and his parents are not surprised that he would, of all topics, choose the one on which he writes in this volume.

Rebecca T. Alpert is a rabbi and associate professor of Religion and Women's Studies at Temple University. She is the author of *Like Bread on the Seder Plate: Jewish Lesbians and the Transformation of Tradition*, co-author of *Exploring Judaism: A Reconstructionist Approach*, and editor of *Voices of the Religious Left: A Contemporary Sourcebook* as well as of numerous articles.

Harry Brod is professor of Philosophy and Humanities at the University of Northern Iowa. He is the co-author of *White Men Challenging Racism: 35 Personal Stories*, editor of *The Making of Masculinities: The New Men's Studies* and *A Mensch among Men: Explorations in Jewish Masculinity*, and co-editor of a forthcoming book on new perspectives on Jewish masculinity. He is an internationally recognized leader in the academic field of masculinity studies and the profeminist men's movement.

Miriyam Glazer is an eclectic scholar, international lecturer, writer, rabbi, and professor of literature at the American Jewish University (formerly the University of Judaism). Her recent books include *Dreaming the Actual: Contemporary Fiction and Poetry by Israeli Women Writers; Dancing on the Edge of the World: Jewish Stories of Faith, Inspiration, and Love;* and, with her sister Phyllis Glazer, the *Essential Book of Jewish Festival Cooking.* Editor of *The Bedside Torah* by Bradley Shavit Artson, she is now completing a spiritual guide to the psalms of the liturgy with David Lieber and a memoir of the last 50 years of Jewish life in Israel and the United States, titled *Judaism, Wars, and Womanhood.*

Adam Goodkind is a graduate of a double bachelor's program at Columbia University and the Jewish Theological Seminary. His primary interest lies in exploring the connections between linguistics and religion.

Robert Karasov has been a pediatrician for over 20 years in a suburb of Minneapolis. He currently has a Bush Medical Fellowship to study psychopharmacology and to improve mental health care delivery. He is also a *mohel* and cantor and serves on his synagogue and Federation Boards of Directors.

Lenny Krayzelburg won four gold medals in swimming at the 2004 Olympics. He has a master's degree in business and now runs the Lenny Krayzelburg Swim School in Los Angeles.

Samuel A. Kunin has been a board-certified urologic surgeon since 1966. He was trained as a *mohel* by Hebrew Union College; and since 1984, he has circumcised many Jewish males of all ages. He has extensively taught people about the medical and religious aspects of *brit milah,* including rabbinical students at the Ziegler School of Rabbinic Studies at the American Jewish University. The beginning sections of his essay in this volume are excerpted and adapted from his 1998 book, *Circumcision: Its Place in Judaism, Past and Present.*

Lori Hope Lefkovitz is the Sadie Gottesman and Arlene Gottesman Reff Professor of Gender and Judaism and director of Kolot: The Center for Jewish Women's and Gender Studies at the Reconstructionist Rabbinical College.

Judith Levitan is a practicing obstetrician/gynecologist in Minneapolis, Minnesota. She received her bachelor's degree at Brandeis University, doctor of medicine at the University of Minnesota, and residency training at a combined program of the University of Minnesota and Hennepin County Medical Center.

Judith Ruskay Rabinor is director of the American Eating Disorders Center with offices on Long Island and in New York City. She is a consultant to the FEGs Eating Disorders Prevention Program, "NoBody's Perfect," of the Renfrew Center Foundation, and is an adjunct professor at Long Island University and a supervisor at the Center for the Study of Anorexia and Bulimia in New York City. She is the author of *A Starving Madness: Tales of Hunger, Hope and Healing in Psychotherapy.*

Abraham J. Twerski is the founder and medical director emeritus of Gateway Rehabilitation Center. He is an international authority in the field of chemical dependency and a frequent lecturer on topics including stress, self-esteem, and spirituality. He is also an ordained rabbi, an associate professor of psychiatry at the University of Pittsburgh School of Medicine, and the author of over 50 books and articles.

Index

Index